JAVA API

REFERENCE

Colin Fraizer

Jill Bond

New
Riders

New Riders Publishing, Indianapolis, Indiana

Java API Reference

By Colin Fraizer and Jill Bond

Published by:
New Riders Publishing
201 West 103rd Street
Indianapolis, IN 46290 USA

Printed in the United States of America 1 2 3 4 5 6 7 8 9 0

CIP data available upon request

Warning and Disclaimer

This book is designed to provide information about the java.awt API package. Every effort has been made to make this book as complete and as accurate as possible, but no warranty or fitness is implied.

The information is provided on an "as is" basis. The author(s) and New Riders Publishing shall have neither liability nor responsibility to any person or entity with respect to any loss or damages arising from the information contained in this book or from the use of the disks or programs that may accompany it.

Publisher	*Don Fowley*
Publishing Manager	*Jim LeValley*
Marketing Manager	*Mary Foote*
Managing Editor	*Carla Hall*

Senior Editor
Sarah Kearns

Development Editor
Chris Cleveland

Associate Marketing Manager
Tamara Apple

Acquisitions Coordinator
Tracy Turgeson

Administrative Coordinator
Karen Opal

Cover Designer
Sandra Schroeder

Cover Production
Aren Howell

Book Designer
Sandra Schroeder

Production Manager
Kelly D. Dobbs

Production Team Supervisor
Laurie Casey

Graphics Image Specialists
Steve Adams
Brad Dixon
Clint Lahnen
Laura Robbins

Production Analysts
Jason Hand
Bobbi Satterfield

Production Team
Dan Caparo
Terrie Deemer
Jennifer Eberhardt
David Garratt
Aleata Howard
Joe Millay
Christy Wagner

Indexer
Chris Cleveland

About the Authors

Colin Fraizer has been designing and developing network applications since 1989. He holds a bachelor of science degree in biochemistry from Indiana University. His interests include collaborative software and the development of client-server systems using corporate intranets. Mr. Fraizer is a senior software engineer with Lexis-Nexis Corporation in Dayton, Ohio.

Jill Bond has been involved in the computer book publishing industry since 1989. She worked in-house at Macmillan Publishing as an indexer and editor, and in 1992, left in-house to work as a freelance editor, developer, and author. Jill received her education from Purdue University in English and Sociology. In addition to writing and developing computer books for Macmillan, she also teaches and writes liturgical music for the Catholic Church, and enjoys reading, bicycling, and Samuel Adams lager beer. Jill lives in Columbus, Indiana, with her husband, Joel, and two daughters, Ashley and Alecia.

Trademark Acknowledgments

All terms mentioned in this book that are known to be trademarks or service marks have been appropriately capitalized. New Riders Publishing cannot attest to the accuracy of this information. Use of a term in this book should not be regarded as affecting the validity of any trademark or service mark.

Dedication

From Colin Fraizer:

To my beloved Kristy, for all her patience and understanding.

From Jill Bond:

For Ashley, Alecia, and Joel

Acknowledgments

From Jill Bond:

When taking on any project, no one person is solely responsible for all aspects of the finished product. The finished product is the culmination of the experience of all those involved. My heartfelt gratitude goes to Carla Hall, Managing Editor at NRP, who saw in me what I could not express (On a clear day...) and to Jim LeValley, for the opportunity offered and the humor shared (Mom, Mom, Mom!). Also, this book would not have been complete without the expertise and eagle eye of Colin Fraizer, the Java guru that he is, and all the folks at NRP, including Chris Cleveland and Sarah Kearns. Mostly, my appreciation goes to my parents, Betty and Chet Bomaster, for their lifelong confidence in me, and to my family, Joel, Ashley, and Alecia, for their inspiration, patience, and continual support.

Contents at a Glance

Table of Contents

10 Color Class   59

13   Dialog Class   111

14   Dimension Class   116

22 GridBagConstraints Class   198

23   GridBagLayout Class   208

Technology Before Java

Only a few short years ago, it seemed almost no one had heard of the Internet; certainly no one outside universities or government work paid it any attention whatsoever. Many of us who were part of the Internet community displayed a certain smugness because we had access to this fabulous resource that corporations and average citizens would *never* understand. Then, along came this fabulous program from the National Center for Supercomputer Applications: NCSA Mosaic. Overnight, the Internet was abuzz with talk of this fabulous World Wide Web that Mosaic was making popular. Then, even more fantastic, the excitement that the WWW generated began to spread beyond the ivy-covered walls of universities—corporate America was taking notice.

References to the Internet began to appear regularly in the *New York Times*, the *Wall Street Journal*, *Newsweek*, and *Time*. The Internet—the Web, in particular—had captured the attention of the popular culture, and the elites were taking notice. The newfound ease of navigating the Internet to read text, view graphics, listen to sound clips, and watch animations was leading millions to explore the Internet, but people wanted more. This easy navigation was nice, but people wanted interactivity. Soon people were using clickable image maps and Web forms to deliver real applications across the Internet. The new citizens of the Net started seeing ways to solve problems, even make money, with the Web.

The problem was that developing applications for the Web was *hard*. These early forms-based programs did not (and could not) have the features and interactive response that people had come to expect from modern applications, generating frustration among both the developers and users of Web applications. If only there were some way to make Web programs more interactive without giving up the advantages of being able to reach PC, Unix, Macintosh, and other users all from the same program. This is when Java entered the picture.

Java was built on the promise of the Web and CGI-based applications, but offered so much more—promising to clear away so many of the frustrations of the early Web developers, to add animation to Web applications, and to work across platforms from the same code. Furthermore, Java looked like C/C++. The thousands of C/C++ programmers that inhabited the Internet found that they understood the basics right away. They were ready to write Java applets and applications.

There is, however, another problem. Although Java's superficial resemblance to C and C++ makes it easy for almost anyone to write programs that perform simple calculations or loop through a repeated task, you must still master the extensive Java applications programming interface (API) to create useful applications or applets. Programmers familiar with the Macintosh, Microsoft Windows, or the X Window System will grasp the essentials right away, but may become bogged down as they struggle with the still very immature API documentation available with the Java Development Kit (JDK). This book attempts to alleviate these problems by providing clarifying material along with example code fragments that demonstrate how each API class's methods should be called.

Who Will Want This Book?

Any programmer who will be developing applets for the Internet will want this book. Those making the transition from more traditional application development and delivery will find this book an indispensable aid. Also, those seeking to expand their repertoire from HTML and CGI programming to include Java applets will delight in the clear descriptions and concise code examples in this book. Our hope is that this book will help applet programmers take full advantage of the java.awt and java.applet APIs and to eliminate much of the frustration that accompanies them due to lack of coherent documentation.

In addition to the applet programmer, the Java *application* programmer who may be totally unconcerned with the Web will find this a useful volume. The nature of Java makes it ideal for those who want to develop cross-platform applications. Unfortunately, this advantage comes at a price in complexity. To make your applications attractive and functional across PC, Macintosh, and Unix platforms will require a good understanding of awt's components, layout managers, and utility classes. The explanations and examples in this book will be a great aid to this understanding.

java.awt Classes Grouped by Function

Layout Managers

BorderLayout class

CardLayout class

FlowLayout class

GridBagLayout class

GridLayout class

Component Classes

Button

Canvas

Checkbox

CheckboxMenuItem

Choice

Container

Dialog

FileDialog

Frame

Label

List

Menu

MenuBar

MenuComponent

MenuContainer

MenuItem

Panel

Scrollbar

continues

TextArea

TextComponent

TextField

Window

Utility Classes

Color

Event

Font

FontMetrics

Graphics

GridBagConstraints

Image

Insets

MediaTracker

Point

Polygon

Rectangle

Toolkit

One of the most exciting areas where Java is gaining a foothold is cut off from the Internet altogether. Java is surging in popularity behind the firewalls of the world's corporations. Two or three years ago, the word "intranet" was a typo; today, it holds an important place in the lexicon of corporate programmers. As companies look for new ways to deliver *internal* applications quickly and cheaply, they are increasingly turning to their existing corporate networks and internal Web infrastructure. Java promises to make the delivery of corporate applications via intranets much more effective. We hope this reference will serve corporate developers well as they pursue Java's benefits.

Why Is This Book Important?

The *Java API Reference* is not a tutorial. Those just getting started in the fascinating world of Java will probably want to pick up one of the many fine books that introduce the language and its facilities, such as *Java!* by Tim Ritchey. Those who already use C or C++ will find that it is immediately (and superficially) familiar, but also that there is much unfamiliar ground to cover, including multithreading, exception handling, and the creation of common data structures in the absence of pointers.

Once these language issues have been mastered and the programmer has obtained general familiarity with the Java APIs, we hope that the *Java API Reference* will be the book kept on the desktop. It is a reference to be used time and again, long after the tutorial has been put away (or lent to some newer Java programmer).

The *Java API Reference* is organized with this scenario in mind. Topics can be accessed via the table of contents, the extensive class and methods index, the thumbtabs, the headers that run across the top of each page, or the topics index. It will become the dog-eared companion of the Java programmer wondering about how to call a method, about the order of a constructor's parameters, or about which superclass contains the method you need.

How Is This Book Organized?

The *Java API Reference* contains two main sections—Part I covers the java.applet package, which is needed to implement the java.awt package; Part II covers the classes and subsequent constructors, methods, and variables of the java.awt package. Within each part, the individual classes are listed alphabetically, with a general description of each class followed by a list of its constructors, methods, class variables, and constants with their syntax. Where warranted, each constructor and method description is accompanied by code examples that demonstrate a possible usage for each.

New Riders Publishing

The staff of New Riders Publishing is committed to bringing you the very best in computer reference material. Each New Riders book is the result of months of work by authors and staff who research and refine the information contained within its covers.

As part of this commitment to you, the NRP reader, New Riders invites your input. Please let us know if you enjoy this book, if you have trouble with the information and examples presented, or if you have a suggestion for the next edition.

Please note, though: New Riders staff cannot serve as a technical resource for Java or for questions about software- or hardware-related problems. Please refer to the documentation that accompanies Java or to the applications' Help systems.

If you have a question or comment about any New Riders book, there are several ways to contact New Riders Publishing. We will respond to as many readers as we can. Your name, address, or phone number will never become part of a mailing list or be used for any purpose other than to help us continue to bring you the best books possible. You can write us at the following address:

New Riders Publishing
Attn: Publisher
201 W. 103rd Street
Indianapolis, IN 46290

If you prefer, you can fax New Riders Publishing at (317) 581-4670.

You can also send electronic mail to New Riders at the following Internet address:

```
ccleveland@newriders.mcp.com
```

New Riders is an imprint of Macmillan Computer Publishing. To obtain a catalog or information, or to purchase any Macmillan Computer Publishing book, call (800) 428-5331.

Thank you for selecting the *Java API Reference*!

Part I

java.applet API Package

Applet Class

The Applet class is necessary to implement the components of the java.awt API package. The following is a visual representation of how the java.applet API package and the Applet class fit into the scheme of things:

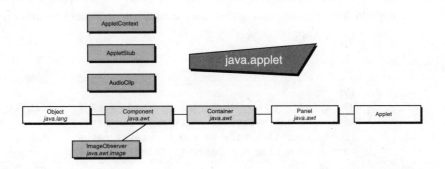

Methods

destroy() method

Syntax:　　　public void destroy()

Description:　The destroy() method enables the applet to clean up (get rid of) the resources (such as threads or running objects) that are being held. If the applet is active, Java stops the applet before the destroy() method takes place.

```
public void destroy() {
    // do clean-up here,
    // such as freeing resources
    // or stopping threads
}
```

getAppletContext() method

Syntax: public AppletContext getAppletContext()

Description: The getAppletContext() method returns a handle to the applet context. The applet context enables an applet to control its environment (usually the browser or the applet viewer).

```
try {
    URL clipUrl = new URL("file:///c:/src/ProRef/test.au");
    AppletContext myContext = getAppletContext();
    // may take advantage of the browser's cache
    AudioClip myClip = myContext.getAudioClip(clipUrl);
    myClip.play();
} catch(MalformedURLException e) {
    showStatus("URL Error.");
}
```

getAppletInfo() method

Syntax: public String getAppletInfo()

Description: The getAppletInfo() method displays information about the author, the applet version, and the applet copyright by returning a string containing that particular information.

```
public String getAppletInfo() {
    return("Test Program v1.0 by Colin Fraizer");
}
```

getAudioClip(URL) method

Syntax: public AudioClip getAudioClip(URL url)

Description: The getAudioClip(URL) method loads an audio clip. After the class has the AudioClip object, you can use the play() method to listen to the audio file.

```
try {
    URL clipUrl = new URL("file:///c:/src/ProRef/test.au");
    AudioClip myClip = getAudioClip(clipUrl);
    myClip.play();
} catch(MalformedURLException e) {
    showStatus("URL Error.");
}
```

getAudioClip(URL, String) method

Syntax: public AudioClip getAudioClip (URL url, String name)

Description: The getAudioClip(URL, String) method loads an audio clip. The URL parameter indicates the location of the object on the World Wide Web. The String parameter indicates the string of the clip you want to get.

```
AudioClip myClip = getAudioClip(getDocumentBase(), "test.au");
myClip.play();
```

getCodeBase() method

Syntax: public URL getCodeBase()

Description: The getCodeBase() method displays a string that represents the directory in which the applet is contained.

getDocumentBase() method

Syntax: public URL getDocumentBase()

Description: The getDocumentBase() retrieves the object that represents the directory of the file from which the applet runs.

```
Image myImage = getImage(getDocumentBase(), "test.gif");
```

getImage(URL) method

Syntax: public Image getImage(URL url)

Description: The getImage(URL) method immediately loads an image object from the specified URL and creates an instance of the Image class. This method always returns some image object, even if the image does not exist. The URL parameter indicates the location of the image or object on the World Wide Web.

```
try {
    myImageUrl = new URL("file:///c:/src/book/ProRef/test.gif");
    myImage = getImage(myImageUrl);
} catch(MalformedURLException e) {
    showStatus("URL Error");
}
```

getImage(URL, String) method

Syntax: public Image getImage(URL url, String name)

Description: The getImage(URL, String) method loads an image object from a specified
                  URL and creates an instance of the Image class. This method also specifies
                  the string that represents the path or file name of the actual image. This
                  method always returns some image object, even if the image does not exist.
                  The URL parameter indicates the location of the object on the World Wide
                  Web. The String parameter indicates the string of the object or image.

```
Image myImage = getImage(getDocumentBase(), "test.gif");
```

getParameter(String) method

Syntax: public String getParameter(String name)

Description: The getParameter(String) method finds the parameter of the applet. This
                  method accepts a specified string (the string that represents the name of the
                  parameter you are looking for) and returns a string that contains a corre-
                  sponding value.

```
String side = getParameter("side");
try {
     int numPlayers =
Integer.parseInt(getParameter("numplayers"));
     textArea.appendText("numplayers is fine\n");
} catch (NumberFormatException e) {
     textArea.appendText("numplayers parameter badly
formatted\n");
}
```

getParameterInfo() method

Syntax: public String[][] getParameterInfo()

Description: The getParameterInfo() method returns an array of strings that describe the
parameters of an applet. The array usually consists of sets of three strings:
the parameter name, the type of value needed for the parameter, and the
description of the parameter.

```
public String[][] getParameterInfo() {
    String[][] myInfo = {
        { "numplayers", "integer", "number of players – one or
        ⮞zero" },
        { "side", "character", "must be character 'X' or 'O'" }
    };

    return(myInfo);
}
```

init() method

Syntax: public void init()

Description: The init() method *initializes* (creates the objects needed, loads images or fonts, and so on) the applet when it is first loaded or reloaded. You do not need to call this method directly—init() is called automatically when the applet is created.

```
// replaces the constructor - only called once
    // called when the applet is created
    public void init() {
        textArea = new TextArea(10, 40);
        this.add(textArea);
        textArea.appendText("Initialized.\n");
        repaint();
        System.err.println("Initializing\n");
    }
```

isActive() method

Syntax: public boolean isActive()

Description: The isActive() method determines whether an applet is active. This method returns True when the applet is active. Java marks an applet active immediately before the start() method is called.

play(URL) method

Syntax: public void play(URL url)

Description: The play(URL) method loads and plays a specified audio clip at a particular URL. If the audio clip you specify is not found, an error message will not appear; however, nothing will play.

```
try {
    URL clipUrl = new URL("file:///c:/src/book/ProRef/test.au");
    play(clipUrl);
} catch(MalformedURLException e) {
    showStatus("URL Error.");
}
```

play(URL, String) method

Syntax: public void play(URL url, String name)

Description: The play(URL, String) loads and plays a specified audio clip at a particular
               URL. The String parameter enables you to further specify a path name. If
               the audio clip you specify is not found, an error message will not appear;
               however, nothing will play.

```
play(getDocumentBase(), "game.au");
```

resize(Dimension) method

Syntax: public void resize(Dimension d)

Description: The resize(Dimension) method assigns new dimensions for a specified
               applet.

```
Dimension dim = new Dimension(width + 10, height + 10);
resize(dim);
```

resize(int, int) method

Syntax: public void resize(int width, int height)

Description: The resize(int, int) method adjusts the size of the applet and ensures that
document formatting will be correct. Although this method works for
AppletViewer, it has no effect when the applet is viewed with Netscape
Navigator.

```
public void paint(Graphics g) {
        Font myFont = new Font("TimesRoman", Font.ITALIC, 24);
        FontMetrics myMetrics = g.getFontMetrics(myFont);

        String myString = "Does resize work in my applet?";
        height = myMetrics.getHeight();
        width = myMetrics.stringWidth(myString);

        resize(width + 10, height + 10);

        g.setFont(myFont);
        g.drawString(myString, 5, height + 5);
}
```

setStub(AppletStub) method

Syntax: public final void setStub(AppletStub stub)

Description: The setStub(AppletStub) method sets the applet stub generated by Java.
Stubs are bits of code that translate arguments and return values between
Java and C. Stubs are set automatically by the system.

showStatus(String) method

Syntax: public void showStatus(String msg)

Description: The showStatus(String) method specifies that applet status messages
appear in the status bar of the browser. You can use this to specify
messages for errors, printing, and so on.

```
showStatus("Your message here.");
```

start() method

Syntax: public void start()

Description: The start() method begins (or starts) the execution of the applet. This
method is called immediately after initialization and is implemented by the
system each time you visit the applet.

```
// called -after- init, can be called multiple times
    public void start() {
        textArea.appendText("Starting.\n");
        repaint();
    }
```

stop() method

Syntax: public void stop()

Description: The stop() method is a system call to stop the applet. Stopping occurs when
the reader leaves a page or the document is no longer on-screen. Because
this is a system method, it is called automatically before the destroy()
method.

```
// called when you leave the page
   public void stop() {
       textArea.appendText("Stopping.\n");
       repaint();
   }
```

Part 2

java.awt API Package

java.awt API Package

The java.awt API package consists predominantly of component classes and layout managers. For organizational purposes, they are listed alphabetically in this book. It is important, however, that the Java programmer understand the interaction and hierarchy of the java.awt API's classes. The component classes are structured as follows:

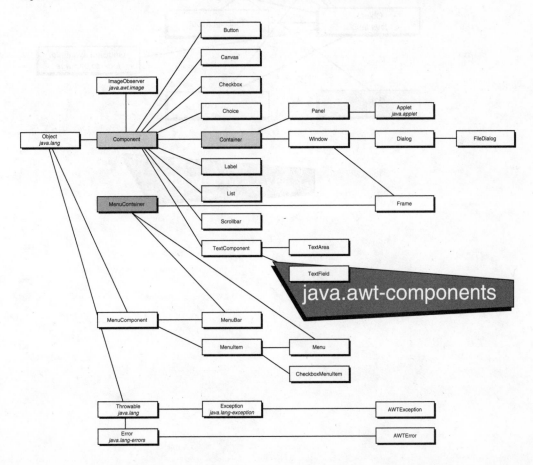

The layout managers that are responsible for organizing java.awt components are structured as follows:

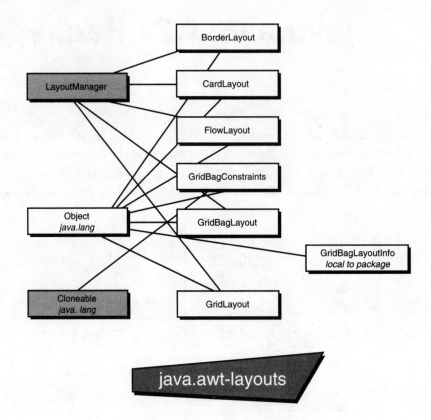

BorderLayout Class

Description: The BorderLayout class is a layout manager class, useful for organizing components in simple windows. For more complex layouts, the GridLayout or GridBagLayout classes should be used. With this layout manager, components are first laid out around the edges of the container: the "North" (top), "South" (bottom), "East" (right side), and "West" (left side). Finally, all remaining space is given to the object in the "Center." You need not specify objects for all four sides of the container; all the leftover space will be used for the "Center" object.

Constructors

BorderLayout() constructor

Syntax: public BorderLayout()

Description: The BorderLayout() constructor specifies a new border layout. You use navigational directions (north, south, east, west) to indicate panel placement.

```
BorderLayout myLayout = new BorderLayout();
this.setLayout(myLayout);
```

BorderLayout(int, int) constructor

Syntax: public BorderLayout(int hgap, int vgap)

Description: The BorderLayout(int, int) constructor specifies horizontal and vertical gaps (in pixels) when creating a new border layout. You use navigational directions (north, south, east, west) to indicate panel placement.

```
this.setLayout(new BorderLayout(5, 5));
```

Methods

addLayoutComponent(String, Component) method

Syntax: public void addLayoutComponent(String name, Component comp)

Description: The addLayoutComponent(String, Component) method specifies individual components to add to a layout. The String parameter indicates the name of the string and the Component parameter indicates the name of the component. You indicate the placement of the component in navigational directions: north, south, east, and west. This method should not be called directly from an application or applet.

layoutContainer(Container) method

Syntax: public void layoutContainer(Container target)

Description: The layoutContainer(Container) method specifies a container to lay out. To satisfy the constraints of the BorderLayout object, the layoutContainer(Container) method reshapes the specified added components in the target container. Do not call this method from an application or applet.

minimumLayoutSize(Container) method

Syntax: public Dimension minimumLayoutSize(Container target)

Description: The minimumLayoutSize(Container) method returns the minimum dimensions required to lay out the components in a specified target. Do not call this method from an application or applet.

preferredLayoutSize(Container) method

Syntax: public Dimension preferredLayoutSize(Container target)

Description: The preferredLayoutSize(Container) method returns the preferred dimensions for a specified layout. The dimensions are determined by the components in the target container you specify.

```
System.err.println("preferred size == " +

Integer.toString(myLayout.preferredLayoutSize(buttonPanel).width)
+ " x " +

Integer.toString(myLayout.preferredLayoutSize(buttonPanel).height));
```

removeLayoutComponent(Component) method

Syntax: public void removeLayoutComponent(Component comp)

Description: The removeLayoutComponent(Component) method removes specified components from a layout. The Component parameter indicates the component you want to remove.

```
myLayout.removeLayoutComponent(myField);
```

toString() method

Syntax: public String toString()

Description: The toString() method returns a string representation of the values of a
                 particular BorderLayout.

```
System.err.println("layout == " + myLayout.toString());
```

Button Class

Description: The Button class is used to display a pushbutton-type component in the applet or application. This button is generally associated with an action that occurs when the user interacts with the button via a mouse click or key press. The current Button class allows only a text string label, unlike many common window toolkits that allow buttons to have a graphical label.

Constructors

Button() constructor

Syntax: public Button()

Description: The Button() constructor creates non-labeled user interface buttons. Actions you specify are triggered when a user clicks on a button created with the Button() constructor.

```
Button myButton = new Button();
myButton.setLabel("Press Me");
```

Button(String) constructor

Syntax: public Button(String label)

Description: The Button(String) constructor creates labeled user interface buttons. Actions you specify are triggered when a user clicks on a button created with the Button() constructor.

```
Button myButton = new Button("Press Me");
```

Methods

addNotify() method

Syntax: public synchronized void addNotify()

Description: The addNotify() method creates the peer (equal) of a button without changing the functionality of the button you are creating.

```
public void addNotify() {
     // called by the system
     // used to create the peer for a custom component
}
```

getLabel() method

Syntax: public String getLabel()

Description: The getLabel() method of the Button class returns the label of the button.

```
Button myButton = new Button("Press Me");
String labelString = myButton.getLabel();
System.out.println("My button's label is " + labelString);
```

paramString() method

Syntax: protected String paramString()

Description: The paramString() method of the Button class returns the parameter string of a specified button.

```
// note: you can only call this from a subclass of Button
Button okButton = new Button("OK");
System.out.println("Parameter String == " +
okButton.paramString());
```

setLabel(String) method

Syntax: public void setLabel(String label)

Description: The setLabel(String) method of the Button class sets the label of a specified button.

```
Button myButton = new Button();
myButton.setLabel("Press Me");
String labelString = myButton.getLabel();
System.out.println("My button's label is " + labelString);
```

Button

Canvas Class

Description: The Canvas class is a generic class that is typically subclassed to provide an area in which to draw. For example, a programmer who wants to implement a Java clock might extend the Canvas class and draw in it the clock's face and hands.

Constructors

Canvas() constructor

Syntax: public Canvas()

Description: The Canvas() constructor creates a *canvas*—a component on which you can draw. Canvases cannot contain other components; however, you can paint on them and use them as backgrounds for animations.

```
Canvas myCanvas = new Canvas();
```

Methods

addNotify() method

Syntax: public synchronized void addNotify()

Description: The addNotify() method of the Canvas class creates a peer (equal) of a canvas. Creating a peer changes the user interface of the canvas without changing the functionality of that particular canvas.

paint(Graphics) method

Syntax: public void paint(Graphics g)

Description: The paint(Graphics) method of the Canvas class paints a canvas in the default background color. The g parameter indicates a specific Graphics window. Typically, you would override this default method to redraw the canvas with the content you specify.

```
public void paint(Graphics g) {
    Font myFont = new Font("TimesRoman", Font.ITALIC, 24);
    FontMetrics myMetrics = g.getFontMetrics(myFont);

    String myString = "Does resize work in my applet?";
    height = myMetrics.getHeight();
    width = myMetrics.stringWidth(myString);

    Dimension dim = new Dimension(width + 10, height + 10);
    resize(dim);

    g.setFont(myFont);
    g.drawString(myString, 5, height + 5);
}
```

Canvas

CardLayout Class

Description: The CardLayout layout manager is useful for managing multiple windows that need not all be visible at the same time. It enables the programmer to combine related windows or dialog boxes into a compact on-screen representation that the user can "tab through" by clicking on the appropriate button. For example, a programmer who wants to implement a Java datebook could have a window for each day of the week, each on a separate "card"—when the user clicks on the "Wednesday" button, the appropriate card is displayed.

Constructors

CardLayout() constructor

Syntax: public CardLayout()

Description: The CardLayout() constructor of the CardLayout class creates "cards," similar to Macintosh HyperCard cards. The components you add to cards are usually panels that do not typically appear on-screen all at once. By viewing cards one at a time, flipping from card to card, you can create slide shows. You also can create different layouts for each card, so that each screen can have its own look.

```
cards = new Panel();
cardLayout = new CardLayout();
cards.setLayout(cardLayout);
cards.add("first", new DummyPanel("This is the first panel"));
cards.add("second", new DummyPanel("This is the second panel"));
cards.add("third", new DummyPanel("This is the third panel"));
```

CardLayout(int, int) constructor

Syntax: public CardLayout(int hgap, int vgap)

Description: The CardLayout(int, int) constructor of the CardLayout class specifies gaps in a card layout you create. The hgap parameter specifies a horizontal gap in a card layout. The vgap parameter specifies a vertical gap in a card layout.

```
CardLayout myLayout = new CardLayout(5, 5);
this.setLayout(myLayout);
```

Methods

addLayoutComponent(String, Component) method

Syntax: public void addLayoutComponent(String name, Component name)

Description: The addLayoutComponent(String, Component) method of the CardLayout class adds a component with a specific name to a card layout. The String parameter indicates the name of the component. The Component parameter indicates the component you want to add. This method of the layout manager is called by the system and should not be called by an applet or application.

first(Container) method

Syntax: public void first(Container parent)

Description: The first(Container) method of the CardLayout class flips to the first card
                 in a card layout. The Container parameter indicates the name of the parent
                 container.

```
case Event.ACTION_EVENT:
    if (e.target == firstButton) {
        cardLayout.show(cards, "first");
    } else if (e.target == secondButton) {
        cardLayout.show(cards, "second");
    } else if (e.target ==thirdButton) {
        cardLayout.show(cards, "third");
    } else {
        return(super.handleEvent(e));
    }
    break;
```

last(Container) method

Syntax: public void last(Container parent)

Description: The last(Container) method of the CardLayout class flips to the last card in
                 a container you specify. The Container parameter indicates the name of the
                 parent container.

```
case Event.KEY_ACTION:
    switch(e.key) {
    case e.LEFT:
        cardLayout.previous(cards);
        break;

    case e.RIGHT:
        cardLayout.next(cards);
        break;

    case e.UP:
        cardLayout.first(cards);
        break;

    case e.DOWN:
        cardLayout.last(cards);
        break;

    default:
        return(super.handleEvent(e));
    }
```

layoutContainer(Container) method

Syntax: public void layoutContainer(Container parent)

Description: The layoutContainer(Container) method of the CardLayout class creates a layout in a specified panel. The Container parameter indicates the name of the parent container. This method of the layout manager is called by the system and should not be called by an applet or application.

minimumLayoutSize(Container) method

Syntax: public Dimension minimumLayoutSize(Container parent)

Description: The minimumLayoutSize(Container) method returns the minimum dimensions needed to lay out components in a specified target container. The Container parameter indicates the name of the parent container. This method of the layout manager is called by the system and should not be called by an applet or application.

next(Container) method

Syntax: public void next(Container parent)

Description: The next(Container) method of the CardLayout class flips to the next card of a specified container. The Container parameter determines the parent container.

```
case Event.KEY_ACTION:
    switch(e.key) {
    case e.LEFT:
        cardLayout.previous(cards);
        break;

    case e.RIGHT:
        cardLayout.next(cards);
        break;

    case e.UP:
        cardLayout.first(cards);
        break;

    case e.DOWN:
        cardLayout.last(cards);
        break;

    default:
        return(super.handleEvent(e));
    }
```

preferredLayoutSize(Container) method

Syntax: public Dimension preferredLayoutSize(Container parent)

Description: The preferredLayoutSize(Container) method of the CardLayout class calculates the dimension size of a specified panel. The Container parameter indicates the name of the parent container. This method of the layout manager is called by the system and should not be called by an applet or application.

previous(Container) method

Syntax: public void previous(Container parent)

Description: The previous(Container) method of the CardLayout class flips to the previous card of a specified container. The Container parameter indicates the name of the parent container.

```
case Event.KEY_ACTION:
    switch(e.key) {
    case e.LEFT:
        cardLayout.previous(cards);
        break;

    case e.RIGHT:
        cardLayout.next(cards);
        break;

    case e.UP:
        cardLayout.first(cards);
        break;

    case e.DOWN:
        cardLayout.last(cards);
        break;

    default:
        return(super.handleEvent(e));
    }
```

removeLayoutComponent(Component) method

Syntax: public void removeLayoutComponent(Component comp)

Description: The removeLayoutComponent(Component) method removes a specified
                 component from a card layout. The Component parameter indicates the
                 component you want to remove. This method of the layout manager is
                 called by the system and should not be called by an applet or application.

show(Container, String) method

Syntax: public void show(Container parent, String name)

Description: The show(Container, String) method of the CardLayout class flips to a
                 specified component name in a targeted container. The Container parameter
                 is the name of the parent container. The String parameter indicates the
                 name of the component.

```
case Event.ACTION_EVENT:
    if (e.target == firstButton) {
        cardLayout.show(cards, "first");
    } else if (e.target == secondButton) {
        cardLayout.show(cards, "second");
    } else if (e.target ==thirdButton) {
        cardLayout.show(cards, "third");
    } else {
        return(super.handleEvent(e));
    }
    break;
```

toString() method

Syntax: public String toString()

Description: The toString() method of the CardLayout class returns the String represen-
                tation of the values of a specified card layout.

```
System.err.println("cardLayout == " +
cardLayout.toString());
```

Checkbox Class

Description: The Checkbox class is used to represent either on/off choices ("Should the font be bold or not bold?") or one of several choices like the buttons on a radio ("Would you like to travel by plane, train, or bus?"). The former case usually involves only single or unrelated checkboxes, while the latter case requires that the checkboxes be grouped together so that only one of the choices can be selected at a time. (One cannot travel simultaneously by plane and by train!)

Constructors

Checkbox() constructor

Syntax: public Checkbox()

Description: The Checkbox() constructor of the Checkbox class creates a checkbox that has no label, no Checkbox group, and is initialized to a False state.

```
Checkbox cBox = new Checkbox();
cBox.setLabel("Check Me");
```

Checkbox(String) constructor

Syntax: public Checkbox(String label)

Description: The Checkbox(String) constructor of the Checkbox class creates a checkbox that has a label you specify, no Checkbox group, and that is initialized to a False state.

```
CheckBox cBox = new Checkbox("Check Me");
```

Checkbox(String, CheckboxGroup, boolean) constructor

Syntax: public Checkbox(String label, CheckboxGroup group, boolean state)

Description: The Checkbox(String, CheckboxGroup, boolean) constructor of the Checkbox class creates a checkbox with a label you specify, a Checkbox group you specify, and a Boolean state you specify. If the Checkbox group you specify is not equal to null, then that checkbox becomes a Checkbox button. If that checkbox becomes a button, then you are limited to setting only one checkbox in a Checkbox group at a time.

```
CheckboxGroup cbGroup = new CheckboxGroup();
cBox = new Checkbox("Check Me", cbGroup, true);
dBox = new Checkbox("No, Check ME", cbGroup, false);
```

Methods

addNotify() method

Syntax: public synchronized void addNotify()

Description: The addNotify() method of the Checkbox class creates the peer (equal) of a specified checkbox. This method creates a peer without changing the functionality of the checkbox. This method of the Checkbox class is called by the system to create a platform-specific representation of this component. It should not be called directly by an application or applet except in a subclass of Checkbox, and then only to override the default addNotify() method.

```
public class NewCheckbox extends Checkbox {
    public synchronized void addNotify() {
        super.addNotify();
        // when we get to here, the peer has been created
    }
}
```

getCheckboxGroup() method

Syntax: public CheckboxGroup getCheckboxGroup()

Description: The getCheckboxGroup() method of the Checkbox class returns the
Checkbox group you specify.

```
CheckboxGroup myGroup = cBox.getCheckboxGroup();
```

getLabel() method

Syntax: public String getLabel()

Description: The getLabel() method of the Checkbox class returns the label of a button.

```
System.out.println("The label for cBox is " +
cBox.getLabel());
```

getState() method

Syntax: public boolean getState()

Description: The getState() method of the Checkbox class returns the Boolean state (True or False) of a specified checkbox.

```
if (cBox.getState() == true) {
    System.err.println("Yeah, you picked me!");
} else if (dBox.getState() == true) {
    System.err.println("Woohoo!  I got picked.");
} else {
    System.err.println("Awwww.  You don't like us.");
}
```

paramString() method

Syntax: protected String paramString()

Description: The paramstring() method of the Checkbox class returns the String parameter of a specified checkbox.

```
System.out.println("Parameter String == " +
cBox.paramString());
```

setCheckboxGroup(CheckboxGroup) method

Syntax: public void setCheckboxGroup(CheckboxGroup g)

Description: The setCheckboxGroup(CheckboxGroup) method of the Checkbox class sets the Checkbox group to a specified group. The g parameter indicates the new Checkbox group.

Checkbox

```
// create the checkbox group
CheckboxGroup cbGroup = new CheckboxGroup();

// create the checkboxes
Checkbox cBox = new Checkbox("Check Me");
Checkbox dBox = new Checkbox("No, Check ME");

// then add them to the group
cBox.setCheckboxGroup(cbGroup);
dBox.setCheckboxGroup(cbGroup);

// and set ONE of them to true
cBox.setState(true);
```

setLabel(String) method

Syntax: public void setLabel(String label)

Description: The setLabel(String) method of the Checkbox class sets a button with a
                 specified label. The String parameter indicates the label you want to use
                 for the button.

```
Checkbox cBox = new Checkbox();
cBox.setState(true);
cBox.setLabel("Check Me");
```

setState(boolean) method

Syntax: public void setState(boolean state)

Description: You use the Checkbox class to create checkboxes, which are user interface components. Checkboxes are Boolean, meaning that they only return True (checked) or False (unchecked). You can also create *nonexclusive checkboxes*—checkboxes in a series in which you can select any or all options.

```
Checkbox cBox = new Checkbox();
cBox.setState(true);
```

Checkbox

CheckboxGroup Class

Description: The CheckboxGroup class provides the capability to group a set of related checkboxes so that only one can be selected at any given time. It implements functionality similar to the buttons on a radio—when you press the button for the classical station, the button for the rock and roll station automatically pops out.

Constructors

CheckboxGroup() constructor

Syntax: public CheckboxGroup()

Description: The CheckboxGroup() constructor of the CheckboxGroup class creates a new Checkbox group.

```
CheckboxGroup cbGroup = new CheckboxGroup();
cBox = new Checkbox("Check Me", cbGroup, true);
dBox = new Checkbox("No, Check ME", cbGroup, false);
```

Methods

getCurrent() method

Syntax: public Checkbox getCurrent

Description: The getCurrent() method of the Checkbox group accesses the currently selected checkbox.

```
if (cbGroup.getCurrent() == cBox) {
    System.err.println("cBox is checked");
} else if (cbGroup.getCurrent() == dBox) {
    System.err.println("dBox is checked");
} else {
    cbGroup.setCurrent(cBox);
}
```

setCurrent(Checkbox) method

Syntax: public synchronized void setCurrent(Checkbox box)

Description: The setCurrent(Checkbox) method sets a specific checkbox to the current
                checkbox. The box parameter indicates the current Checkbox choice.

```
if (cbGroup.getCurrent() == cBox) {
    System.err.println("cBox is checked");
} else if (cbGroup.getCurrent() == dBox) {
    System.err.println("dBox is checked");
} else {
    cbGroup.setCurrent(cBox);
}
```

CheckboxGroup

toString() method

Syntax: public String toString()

Description: The toString() method of the CheckboxGroup class returns the String
                representation of the values of the CheckboxGroup you specify.

```
System.out.println("The string representatino of cbGroup is " +
    cbGroup.toString());
```

CheckboxMenuItem Class

Description: The CheckboxMenuItem class provides the same functionality as a checkbox, but can be used on a menu.

Constructors

CheckboxMenuItem(String) constructor

Syntax: public CheckboxMenuItem(String label)

Description: The CheckboxMenuItem(String) constructor of the CheckboxMenuItem class creates a Checkbox item and specifies a label for that Checkbox item. The String parameter indicates the label.

```
MenuBar menuBar = new MenuBar();

// the style menu
Menu style = new Menu("Style");
style.add(new CheckboxMenuItem("Bold"));
style.add(new CheckboxMenuItem("Italic"));
style.add(new CheckboxMenuItem("Subscript"));

// put the menu on the menubar
menuBar.add(style);

this.setMenuBar(menuBar);
```

Methods

addNotify() method

Syntax: public synchronized void addNotify()

Description: The addNotify() method of the CheckboxMenuItem class creates a peer of
a specified Checkbox item. Creating a peer changes the appearance of the
Checkbox item without changing the functionality of the item.

getState() method

Syntax: public boolean getState()

Description: The getState() method of the CheckboxMenuItem class returns the state
(True or False) of a specified menu item. You can only use this method for
a checkbox.

```
public boolean handleEvent(Event e) {
    if (e.id == Event.ACTION_EVENT) {
        if (e.target == bold) {
            if (bold.getState() == true) {
                System.err.println("You turned ON bold.");
            } else {
                System.err.println("You turned OFF bold.");
            }
        } else {
            return(super.handleEvent(e));
        }
    }
    return(true);
}
```

CheckboxMenuItem

paramString() method

Syntax: public String paramString()

Description: The paramString() method of the CheckboxMenuItem class returns the
String parameter of a specified button.

```
System.err.println("paramString == " +
bold.paramString());
```

setState(boolean) method

Syntax: public void setState(boolean t)

Description: The setState(boolean) method of the CheckboxMenuItem class sets the
state of a specified menu item, providing that the menu item is a checkbox.

```
MenuBar menuBar = new MenuBar();

// the style menu
Menu style = new Menu("Style");
style.add(bold = new CheckboxMenuItem("Bold"));
bold.setState(true);
style.add(italic = new CheckboxMenuItem("Italic"));
style.add(subscript = new CheckboxMenuItem("Subscript"));

// put the menu on the menubar
menuBar.add(style);

this.setMenuBar(menuBar);
```

Choice Class

Description: The Choice class provides the capability to present a list of choices, represented graphically as a pop-up menu, to the user. One of the items in the list is the "selected item," which is displayed as the Choice component's label.

Constructors

Choice() constructor

Syntax: public Choice()

Description: The Choice() constructor of the Choice class creates or constructs a new menu item and positions it according to your specifications.

```
Choice myChoice = new Choice();
myChoice.addItem("Big");
myChoice.addItem("Bigger");
myChoice.addItem("Biggest");
```

Methods

addItem(String) method

Syntax: public synchronized void addItem(String item)

Description: The addItem(String) method of the Choice class adds a menu item to a menu. The String parameter indicates the menu item you want to add.

```
Choice myChoice = new Choice();
myChoice.addItem("Big");
myChoice.addItem("Bigger");
myChoice.addItem("Biggest");
```

addNotify() method

Syntax: public synchronized void addNotify()

Description: The addNotify() method of the Choice class creates a peer of the choice you specify. The peer modifies the appearance of the choice without changing the functionality of the choice.

countItems() method

Syntax: public int countItems()

Description: The countItems() method of the Choice class returns the number of items available in the choice you specify.

```
myChoice = new Choice();
myChoice.addItem("Big");
myChoice.addItem("Bigger");
myChoice.addItem("Biggest");
try {
    // select the last item
    myChoice.select(myChoice.countItems() - 1);
} catch(IllegalArgumentException e) {
    ;
}
```

getItem(int) method

Syntax: public String getItem(int index)

Description: The getItem() method of the Choice class returns the string at the index you specify in that particular choice. The index parameter indicates the index from which you want to begin.

```
myChoice = new Choice();
myChoice.addItem("Big");
myChoice.addItem("Bigger");
myChoice.addItem("Biggest");
try {
    // select the last item
    myChoice.select(myChoice.countItems() - 1);
    System.err.println("The last item is " +
        myChoice.getItem(myChoice.countItems() - 1));
} catch(IllegalArgumentException e) {
    ;
}
```

getSelectedIndex() method

Syntax: public int getSelectedIndex()

Description: The getSelectedIndex() method of the Choice class returns the index of the item you currently have selected.

```
public boolean handleEvent(Event e) {
    if (e.id == Event.ACTION_EVENT) {
        if (e.target == myChoice) {
            System.err.println("You selected " +
                myChoice.getItem(myChoice.getSelectedIndex())));
        } else {
            return(super.handleEvent(e));
        }
    }
    return(true);
}
```

getSelectedItem() method

Syntax: public String getSelectedItem()

Description: The getSelectedItem() method of the Choice class returns a string representation of the choice you currently have selected.

```
public boolean handleEvent(Event e) {
    if (e.id == Event.ACTION_EVENT) {
        if (e.target == myChoice) {
            System.err.println("You selected " +
                myChoice.getSelectedItem());
        } else {
            return(super.handleEvent(e));
        }
    }
    return(true);
}
```

paramString() method

Syntax: protected String paramString()

Description: The paramString() method of the Choice class returns the parameter String
of the choice you specify.

select(int) method

Syntax: public synchronized void select(int pos)

Description: The select(int) method of the Choice class selects a menu item from a
specified position. The int parameter indicates the position of the menu
item.

```
Choice myChoice = new Choice();
myChoice.addItem("Big");
myChoice.addItem("Bigger");
myChoice.addItem("Biggest");
try {
    myChoice.select(2);
} catch(IllegalArgumentException e) {
    ;
}
```

select(String) method

Syntax: public void select(String str)

Description: The select(String) method of the Choice class selects the item that has the string you specify. The String parameter indicates the string you are trying to access.

```
myChoice = new Choice();
myChoice.addItem("Big");
myChoice.addItem("Bigger");
myChoice.addItem("Biggest");
// make "Bigger" the default choice
myChoice.select("Bigger");
```

Color Class

Description: The Color class encapsulates the platform-specific information for dealing
with colors. This class provides a cross-platform interface that enables the
programmer to specify colors without knowing the details of the display
hardware on which the application or applet will run.

Constructors

Color(float, float, float) constructor

Syntax: public Color(float r, float g, float b)

Description: The Color(float, float, float) constructor of the Color class creates a color
by specifying red, green, and blue values in the given range (0.0 through
1.0). The actual color Java uses in rendering depends on locating the best
match for the available color space for a given output device. The color
Java uses in rendering depends on finding the best match. The r parameter
indicates the red component. The g parameter indicates the green component. The b parameter indicates the blue component.

```
Color myBlue = new Color(0.0, 0.0, 1.0);
```

Color(int) constructor

Syntax: public Color(int rgb)

Description: The Color(int) constructor of the Color class creates a color using the RGB (red, blue, green) values you specify. Bits 0 through 7 are blue; bits 8 through 15 are green; bits 16 through 23 are red. The actual color Java uses in rendering depends on locating the best match for the available color space for a given output device. The rgb parameter indicates the combined RGB components.

```
Color myRed = new Color(0xFF000000);
```

Color(int, int, int) constructor

Syntax: public Color(int r, int g, int b)

Description: The Color(int, int, int) constructor creates a color using RBG (red, blue, green) values from 0 to 255, or 0.0 to 1.0. The actual color Java uses in rendering depends on locating the best match for the available color space for a given output device. The r parameter indicates red. The g parameter indicates green. The b parameter indicates blue.

```
Color myBlue = new Color(0, 0, 1);
```

Methods

brighter() method

Syntax: public Color brighter()

Description: The brighter() method of the Color class returns a brighter version of a specified color. You might want to use the brighter() method when creating a palette of colors to get brighter variations of the core color you are using.

```
Color brighterColor = myColor.brighter();
```

darker() method

Syntax: public Color darker()

Description: The darker() method of the Color class returns a darker version of a
                 specified color. You might want to use the darker() method when creating a
                 palette of colors to get darker variations of the core color you are using.

```
Color darkerColor = myColor.darker();
```

equals(Object) method

Syntax: public boolean equals(Object obj)

Description: The equals(Object) method of the Color class compares two objects that
                 you specify. Because this method is Boolean, it returns True if the objects
                 are the same and False if the two objects being compared are different. The
                 obj parameter indicates the object with which you want to compare.

```
Color myRed = Color.getColor("red", 0xffff0000);
Color theirRed = Color.getColor("red", Color.blue);
// gets blue, not red
if (myRed.equals(theirRed)) {
    System.err.println("myRed == theirRed");
} else {
    // should print this one
    System.err.println("myRed != theirRed");
}
```

Color

getBlue() method

Syntax:　　　public int getBlue()

Description:　The getBlue() method of the Color class returns the blue component of a specified color.

```
int bluePart = myColor.getBlue();
```

getColor(String) method

Syntax:　　　public static Color getColor(String nm, int v)

Description:　The getColor(String) method of the Color class returns a new Color property you specify. The nm parameter indicates the name of the Color property. The v parameter indicates the value of the color.

getColor(String, Color) method

Syntax:　　　public static Color getColor(String nm, Color v)

Description:　The getColor(String, Color) method of the Color class returns a Color property you specify from a particular color. The nm parameter indicates the name of the Color property. The v parameter indicates the color value.

```
Color myRed = Color.getColor("red", 0xffff0000);
g.setColor(myRed);
g.drawString(myString, 5, height + 5);
```

getColor(String, int) method

Syntax: public static Color getColor(String nm, int v)

Description: The getColor(String, int) method of the Color class returns a Color property you specify from a particular Color value. This method returns the new color. The nm parameter indicates the name of the Color property. The v parameter indicates the value of the color.

getGreen() method

Syntax: public int getGreen()

Description: The getGreen() method of the Color class returns the green component of a specified color.

```
int greenValue = myColor.getGreen();
```

getHSBColor(float, float, float) method

Syntax: public static Color getHSBColor (float h, float s, float b)

Description: The getHSBColor(float, float, float) method of the Color class returns a Color object of HSB values that correspond to an RGB color you specify. The h parameter indicates *hue* or tint of a color. The s parameter indicates *saturation* or color purity. The b parameter indicates the brightness of a color.

Color

```
Color myRed = Color.getHSBColor(1.0, 0.0, 0.0);
```

getRed() method

Syntax: public int getRed()

Description: The getRed() method of the Color class returns the red component of a specified color.

```
int redPart = myColor.redPart();
```

getRGB() method

Syntax: public int getRGB()

Description: The public int getRGB() method of the Color class returns the RGB (red, green, blue) value that represents the color in the default RGB Color Model. Bits 0 through 7 are blue. Bits 8 through 15 are green. Bits 16 through 23 are red. Bits 24 through 31 are 0xff.

```
int rgbValue = myColor.getRGB();
int myRed = rgbValue & 0x00FF0000;
int myGreen = rgbValue & 0x0000FF00;
int myBlue = rgbValue & 0x000000FF;
```

hashCode() method

Syntax: public int hashCode()

Description: Java provides a hash code (a unique number) for each object. Hash codes
are used for storing objects in hash tables. The hashCode() method of the
Color class returns the hash code for an object you specify.

HSBtoRGB(float, float, float) method

Syntax: public static int HSBtoRGB(float hue, float saturation, float brightness)

Description: The HSBtoRGB(float, float, float) method of the Color class returns
the RGB value (this is defined by the RGB ColorModel default) of the
color that corresponds to the HSB (hue, saturation, brightness) color
components. The hue parameter indicates the hue of the component color.
The saturation parameter indicates the saturation of the color. The brightness parameter indicates the brightness of the color.

```
Color myColor = Color.getColor("red", HSBtoRGB(0, 1, 1));
```

RGBtoHSB method

Syntax: public static float[] RGBtoHSB(int r, int g, int b, float hsbvals[])

Description: The RGBtoHSB method of the Color class returns the array that stores
the HSB (hue, saturation, brightness) values that correspond to the color
defined by the RGB (red, green, blue) components. The r parameter
indicates the red component of the color. The g parameter indicates the

Color

green component of the color. The b parameter indicates the blue component of the color. The hsbvals parameter indicates the array you want to use to return the three HSB (hue, saturation, brightness) values.

```
float[] hsbArray = new float[3];
Color.RGBtoHSB(0xFF, 0x00, 0x00, hsbArray);
System.err.println("HSB == " + Float.toString(hsbArray[0]) + " " +
    Float.toString(hsbArray[1]) + " " +
Float.toString(hsbArray[2]));
```

toString() method

Syntax: public String toString()

Description: The toString() method of the Color class returns a string representation of a specified color value.

```
System.out.println("Color String == " +
myColor.toString());
```

Variables

cyan variable

Syntax: public final static Color cyan

Description: The cyan variable of the Color class returns the color cyan.

black variable

Syntax: public final static Color black

Description: The black variable of the Color class returns the color black.

blue variable

Syntax: public final static Color blue

Description: The blue variable of the Color class returns the color blue.

darkGray variable

Syntax: public final static Color darkGray

Description: The darkGray variable of the Color class returns the color dark gray.

gray variable

Syntax: public final static Color gray

Description: The gray variable of the Color class returns the color gray.

Color

green variable

Syntax: public final static Color green

Description: The green variable of the Color class returns the color green.

lightGray variable

Syntax: public final static Color lightGray

Description: The lightGray variable of the Color class returns the color light gray.

magenta variable

Syntax: public final static Color magenta

Description: The magenta variable of the Color class returns the color magenta.

orange variable

Syntax: public final static Color orange

Description: The orange variable of the Color class returns the color orange.

pink variable

Syntax: public final static Color pink

Description: The pink variable of the Color class returns the color pink.

red variable

Syntax: public final static Color red

Description: The red variable of the Color class returns the color red.

white variable

Syntax: public final static Color white

Description: The white variable of the Color class returns the color white.

yellow variable

Syntax: public final static Color yellow

Description: The yellow variable of the Color class returns the color yellow.

Color

Component Class

Description: The Component class creates and nests objects that are components (on-screen items), such as windows, title and menu bars, and so on. You also use this class to create and manage user interface items, such as menu choices, buttons, and lists. In addition, you can use the Component class to group items using containers, such as panels and windows.

Methods

action(Event, Object) method

Syntax: public boolean action(Event evt, Object what)

Description: The action(Event, Object) method of the Component class determines that an action in a specific component is taking place (True). The evt parameter indicates the event within that component, and the what parameter indicates the particular action that is taking place within the component you specify.

```
public boolean action(Event e, Object o) {
    if (e.target == myObj) {
        // process the event here
        return(true);
    } else {
        return(false);
    }
}
```

addNotify() method

Syntax: public void addNotify()

Description: The addNotify() method of the Component class instructs the component you specify to create a peer. Using the addNotify() method creates a peer of the component without changing the functionality.

bounds() method

Syntax: public Rectangle bounds()

Description: Using the bounds() method of the Component class returns the current bounds of a specified component.

```
Rectangle myBounds = checkbox.bounds();
```

checkImage(Image, ImageObserver) method

Syntax: public int checkImage(Image image, ImageObserver)

Description: The checkImage(Image, ImageObserver) method of the Component class determines the construction status of a screen representation of a specified image. The checkImage(Image, ImageObserver) method, however, does not cause the image to begin to load.

Component

checkImage(Image, int, int, ImageObserver) method

Syntax: public int checkImage(Image image, int width, int height, ImageObserver observer)

Description: The checkImage(Image, int, int, ImageObserver) method of the Component class determines the construction status of a representation of a scaled screen of a specified image. The image parameter indicates the image for which you want to check the status. The width parameter indicates the width of the scaled version for which you want to check the status. The height parameter indicates the height of the scaled version for which you want to check the status. The observer parameter indicates the ImageObserver object you want to notify while the image is being prepared. This method returns the Boolean OR of the flags for the available data.

createImage(ImageProducer) method

Syntax: public Image createImage(ImageProducer producer)

Description: The createImage(ImageProducer) method of the Component class creates an image from the image producer you specify. The producer parameter indicates the ImageProducer you specify.

createImage(int, int) method

Syntax: public Image createImage(int width, int height)

Description: The createImage(int, int) method of the Component class creates an off-screen drawable image that you use for double buffering. The width parameter specifies the width of the image, and the height parameter specifies the height of the image.

deliverEvent(Event) method

Syntax: public void deliverEvent(Event e)

Description: The deliverEvent(Event) method of the Component class delivers an event
to a specified component or subcomponent. The e parameter indicates the
event.

```
textField.deliverEvent(e);
```

disable() method

Syntax: public synchronized void disable()

Description: The disable() method of the Component class specifies that a component is
not to respond to user input. You might want to disable a component, such
as a button or menu item.

```
selectors.add(firstButton = new Button("First"));
selectors.add(secondButton = new Button("Second"));
secondButton.disable(); // "gray out" this button
selectors.add(thirdButton = new Button("Third"));
```

enable() method

Syntax: public synchronized void enable()

Description: You use the enable() method of the Component class to enable a specified
component.

Component

```
Button forward = new Button("Forward");
Button back = new Button("Back");
back.disable();
// ...
back.enable();
```

enable(boolean) method

Syntax: public void enable(boolean cond)

Description: The enable(boolean) method of the Component class conditionally enables
a component. If the condition is True, for example, the component is
enabled. If the condition is False, then the component is disabled.

```
Button forward = new Button("Forward");
Button back = new Button("Back");
back.enable(false);
// ...
back.enable(true);
```

getBackground() method

Syntax: public Color getBackground()

Description: The getBackground() method of the Component class returns the background color of a specified component. The background color of the parent
component is returned when the specified component does not have a
background color.

```
Color bgColor = buttonPanel.getBackground();
fieldPanel.setBackground(bgColor);
```

getColorModel method

Syntax: public synchronized ColorModel getColorModel()

Description: The getColorModel method of the Component class accesses the color
model used to display the component on the output device.

```
ColorModel cm = myButton.getColorModel();
```

getFont() method

Syntax: public Font getFont()

Description: The getFont() method of the Component class accesses the font of a
specified component. The font of the parent component is returned when
the specified component does not have a font.

```
Font f = g.getFont();
```

getFontMetrics(Font) method

Syntax: public FontMetrics getFontMetrics (Font font)

Component

Description: The getFontMetrics(Font) accesses the font metrics for a specified component. If the specified component currently is not on-screen, this method
returns null. The font parameter indicates the font you want to access.

```
public void paint(Graphics g) {
        Font myFont = new Font("TimesRoman", Font.ITALIC, 24);
        FontMetrics myMetrics = g.getFontMetrics(myFont);

        String myString = "Does resize work in my applet?";
        height = myMetrics.getHeight();
        width = myMetrics.stringWidth(myString);

        resize(width + 10, height + 10);

        g.setFont(myFont);
        g.drawString(myString, 5, height + 5);
}
```

getForeground() method

Syntax: public Color getForeground()

Description: The getForeground() method of the Component class returns the foreground color of a specified component. The foreground color of the parent
component is returned when the specified component does not have a
foreground color.

```
Color buttonColor = firstButton.getForeground();
secondButton.setForeground(buttonColor);
```

getGraphics() method

Syntax: public Graphics getGraphics()

Description: The getGraphics() method of the Component class returns a Graphics context for a specified component. If the specified component currently is not on-screen, the method returns null.

```
Graphics g = myFrame.getGraphics();
g.drawString(myString, 10, 10);
```

getParent() method

Syntax: public Container getParent()

Description: The getParent() method of the Component class returns the parent of a specified component.

```
buttonPanel = firstButton.getParent();
buttonPanel.add(newButton = new Button("Click Here");
```

getPeer() method

Syntax: public ComponentPeer getPeer()

Description: The getPeer() method of the Component class returns the peer of a specified component.

getToolkit() method

Syntax: public Toolkit getToolkit()

Component

Description: The getToolkit() method of the Component class returns the toolkit of a specified component. You use the toolkit to create a peer for the component you specified in the method.

```
Toolkit myToolkit = myFrame.getToolkit();
Image myImage = myToolkit.getImage("test.gif");
```

gotFocus(Event, Object) method

Syntax: public boolean gotFocus(Event evt, Object what)

Description: The gotFocus(Event, Object) method of the Component class indicates that a specified component has received the input focus. The evt parameter indicates the action you want to take place. The what parameter indicates the object you specify on which the action is taking place.

```
public boolean gotFocus(Event e, Object what) {
    if (what.equals(textField)) {
        // do something here
        return(true);
    } else {
        return(false);
    }
}
```

handleEvent(Event) method

Syntax: public boolean handleEvent(Event evt)

Description: The handleEvent(Event) method of the Component class is a Boolean method that handles (or traps) a specified event to the component. This method returns True when the event is handled and should not be passed to the parent of the specified component. To support the programmer, the default event handler calls some helper methods. The evt parameter indicates the event you want handled.

```java
public boolean handleEvent(Event e) {
    switch(e.id) {

    case Event.ACTION_EVENT:
        if (e.target == firstButton) {
            cardLayout.show(cards, "first");
        } else {
            return(super.handleEvent(e));
        }
        break;

    case Event.KEY_ACTION:
        switch(e.key) {
        case e.LEFT:
            cardLayout.previous(cards);
            break;

        case e.RIGHT:
            cardLayout.next(cards);
            break;

        default:
            return(super.handleEvent(e));
        }

    default:
        return(super.handleEvent(e));
    }
    return(true);
}
```

Component

hide() method

Syntax: public synchronized void hide()

Description: The hide() method of the Component class hides (not displays) a specified
                     component.

```
selectors.add(firstButton = new Button("First"));
selectors.add(secondButton = new Button("Second"));
secondButton.hide(); // don't show this one
selectors.add(thirdButton = new Button("Third"));
```

imageUpdate(Image, int, int, int, int, int) method

Syntax: public boolean imageUpdate(Image img, int flags, int x, int y, int w, int h)

Description: The imageUpdate(Image, int, int, int, int, int) method of the Component
                     class repaints a specified component after the image changes. The method
                     returns True if the image has changed and returns False if the image has not
                     changed. The parameters specify the image, flags, x and y coordinates, and
                     height and width. You will not call this method yourself—it is part of the
                     ImageObserver interface. It will be called by the ImageObserver class.

```
public boolean ImageUpdate(Image, int flags, int x, int y,
      int width, int height) {
      // check the flags to see if you have changes to make
      // add your code to repaint the image here
}
```

inside(int, int) method

Syntax: public synchronized boolean inside(int x, int y)

Description: The inside(int, int) method of the Component class determines whether a specified location using the x and y parameters is within a particular component (True). When the x and y coordinates are within the bounding box of the specified component, the coordinates are inside that component by default.

```
if (checkBox.inside(53, 6)) {
    System.err.println("I'm in!");
}
if (checkBox.inside(20, 0)) {
    System.err.println("I'm not");
}
```

invalidate() method

Syntax: public void invalidate()

Description: The invalidate() method of the Component class invalidates a component.

isEnabled() method

Syntax: public boolean isEnabled()

Description: The isEnabled() method of the Component class enables (True) a component. Unless you specify otherwise (False), components initially are enabled.

Component

```
if (checkBox.isEnabled()) {
    System.err.println("The checkBox is enabled");
}
```

isShowing() method

Syntax: public boolean isShowing()

Description: The isShowing() method of the Component class checks whether a specified component is displayed on-screen. For this to be True (visible on-
screen), the component must be in a container that appears on-screen.

```
if (checkBox.isShowing()) {
    System.err.println("checkBox is showing.");
}
```

isValid() method

Syntax: public boolean isValid()

Description: The isValid() method of the Component class determines whether a component is valid (True). When components first appear on-screen, they are
invalid.

```
if (checkBox.isValid()) {
    System.err.println("checkBox is valid.");
}
```

isVisible() method

Syntax: public boolean isVisible()

Description: The isVisible() method of the Component class checks whether a specified component is visible (True). With the exception of top-level components, such as Frame and Dialog, components initially are visible.

```
if (checkBox.isVisible()) {
    System.err.println("checkBox is visible.");
}
```

keyDown(Event, int) method

Syntax: public boolean keyDown(Event evt, int key)

Description: The keyDown(Event, int) method of the Component class is called when a user presses down a key on the keyboard. The evt parameter indicates the event, and the key parameter indicates the key that is being pressed.

```
public boolean keyDown(Event e, int key) {
    if (key == Event.UP) {
        System.err.println("You pressed UP");
        return(true);
    } else {
        return(false);
    }
}
```

keyUp(Event, int) method

Syntax: public boolean keyUp(Event evt, int key)

Description: The keyUp(Event, int) method of the Component class is called when the user releases a keyboard key that he or she pressed. The evt parameter indicates the event, and the key parameter indicates the key that is being released.

```
public boolean keyUp(Event e, int key) {
    if (key == Event.UP) {
        System.err.println("You released the UP key");
        return(true);
    } else {
        return(false);
    }
}
```

Layout() method

Syntax: public void layout()

Description: The Layout() method of the Component class lays out the component. This value usually is called when the component is validated or established.

list() method

Syntax: public void list()

Description: The list() method of the Component class prints a listing to a print stream.

```
Button myButton = new Button("Press Me");
myButton.list();
```

list(PrintStream) method

Syntax: public void list(PrintStream out)

Description: The list(PrintStream) method of the Component class prints a list to a specified print stream. The out parameter indicates the name of the stream.

```
Button myButton = new Button("Press Me");
myButton.list(System.err);
```

list(PrintStream, int) method

Syntax: public void list(PrintStream out, int indent)

Description: The list(PrintStream) method of the Component class prints a list to a specified print stream, starting at the indentation you specify. The out parameter indicates the name of the stream, and the indent parameter indicates the start of the list.

```
Button myButton = new Button("Press Me");
myButton.list(System.err, 5);
```

Component

locate(int, int) method

Syntax: public Component locate(int x, int y)

Description: The locate(int, int) method of the Component class specifies the return of the component or subcomponent that contains the x, y location. The x parameter indicates the x coordinate, and the y parameter indicates the y coordinate of the component or subcomponent being returned.

```
System.err.println("Component at 52, 5 == " +
    (firstPanel.locate(52, 5)).toString());
```

location() method

Syntax: public Point location()

Description: The location() method of the Component class returns the current location of a specified component. The location of the component is in the coordinate space of the parent component.

```
Point loc = checkBox.location();
System.err.println("Location == " + Integer.toString(loc.x) + "
➡x " +
    Integer.toString(loc.y));
```

lostFocus(Event, Object) method

Syntax: public boolean lostFocus(Event evt, Object what)

Description: The lostFocus(Event, Object) method of the Component class determines whether a specified component has lost input focus (True). The evt parameter indicates the event, and the what parameter indicates the action.

```
public boolean lostFocus(Event e, Object what) {
    if (what.equals(textField)) {
        // do something here
        return(true);
    } else {
        return(false);
    }
}
```

minimumSize() method

Syntax: public Dimension minimumSize()

Description: The minimumSize() method of the Component class returns the minimum size of a specified component.

```
Dimension dim = buttonPanel.minimumSize();
buttonPanel.resize(dim);
```

mouseDown(Event, int, int) method

Syntax: public boolean mouseDown(Event evt, int x, int y)

Description: The mouseDown(Event, int, int) method of the Component class determines whether the mouse is being moved down. The evt parameter indicates the event, the x parameter indicates the x coordinate at the time of the event, and the y parameter indicates the y coordinate at the time of the event.

Component

```
public boolean mouseDown(Event e, int x, int y) {
    // react to the mouse down here
    return(true);
}
```

mouseDrag(Event, int, int) method

Syntax:　　public boolean mouseDrag(Event evt, int x, int y)

Description:　The mouseDrag(Event, int, int) method of the Component class is called when a user presses down a mouse button (True) and drags the mouse. The evt parameter indicates the event taking place. The x parameter indicates the x coordinate. The y parameter indicates the y coordinate.

```
public boolean mouseDrag(Event e, int x, int y) {
    System.err.println("Dragged coordinates == (" +
    ➥Integer.toString(x) +
        "," + Integer.toString(y) + ")");
    return(true);
}
```

mouseEnter(Event, int, int) method

Syntax:　　public boolean mouseEnter(Event evt, int x , int y)

Description:　The mouseEnter(Event, int, int) method of the Component class determines that the mouse pointer has entered a specified component (True). The evt parameter indicates the event. The x parameter indicates the x coordinate of the mouse at the time of the event. The y parameter indicates the y coordinate of the mouse at the time of the event.

```
public boolean mouseEnter(Event e, int x, int y) {
    // react to the mouse enter here
    return(true);
}
```

mouseExit(Event, int, int) method

Syntax: public boolean mouseExit(Event evt, int x, int y)

Description: The mouseExit(Event, int, int) method of the Component class determines
that the mouse has left (or exited) a specified component (True). The evt
parameter indicates the event. The x parameter indicates the x coordinate of
the mouse at the time of the event. The y parameter indicates the y coordinate of the mouse at the time of the event.

```
public boolean mouseExit(Event e, int x, int y) {
    // react to the mouse exit here
    return(true);
}
```

mouseMove(Event, int, int) method

Syntax: public boolean mouseMove(Event evt, int x, int y)

Description: The mouseMove(Event, int, int) method of the Component class determines that the user has moved the mouse (True). The evt parameter indicates the event. The x parameter indicates the x coordinate of the mouse
pointer at the time of the event. The y parameter indicates the y coordinate
of the mouse pointer at the time of the event.

Component

```
public boolean mouseMove(Event e, int x, int y) {
    // react to the mouse move here
    return(true);
}
```

mouseUp(Event, int, int) method

Syntax: public boolean mouseUp(Event evt, int x, int y)

Description: The mouseUp(Event, int, int) method of the Component class determines when or whether the user is moving the mouse up (True). The x parameter indicates the x coordinate of the mouse pointer at the time of the event. The y parameter indicates the y coordinate of the mouse pointer at the time of the event.

```
public boolean mouseUp(Event e, int x, int y) {
    // react to the mouse up here
    return(true);
}
```

move(int, int) method

Syntax: public void move(int x, int y)

Description: The move(int, int) method of the Component class moves a specified component to a new location. The x parameter indicates the x coordinate in the coordinate space of the parent component. The y parameter indicates the y coordinate in the coordinate space of the parent component.

```
checkBox.move(26,5);
```

nextFocus() method

Syntax: public void next Focus()

Description: The nextFocus() method of the Component class moves the focus to the next component you specify.

```
checkBox.nextFocus();
```

paint(Graphics) method

Syntax: public void paint(Graphics g)

Description: The paint(Graphics) method of the Component class paints the active component. The g parameter indicates the graphics window you specify.

```
public void paint(Graphics g) {
    // renew the display here
    g.drawString(myString, 5, height + 5);
}
```

paintAll(Graphics) method

Syntax: public void paintAll(Graphics g)

Component

Description: The paintAll(Graphics) method of the Component class paints the component and its specified subcomponents. The g parameter indicates the graphics window in which the component and subcomponents are located.

```
firstPanel.paintAll(firstPanel.getGraphics());
```

paramString() method

Syntax: protected String paramString()

Description: The paramString() method of the Component class returns the parameter String of a specified component.

```
System.out.println("The button's parameter string is " +
    myButton.paramString());
```

postEvent(Event) method

Syntax: public void postEvent(Event e)

Description: The postEvent(Event) method of the Component class posts an event (or action) to a specified component. Using this method results in a call to the handleEvent method. The event (or action) is passed on to the parent of a specified component when the handleEvent method returns False. The e parameter indicates the event (or action) you specify.

```
button.postEvent(e);
```

preferredSize() method

Syntax: public Dimension preferredSize()

Description: The preferredSize() method of the Component class sizes the component to
the dimension you want. This method is used by the LayoutManager
interface and would not typically be defined by a user class.

prepareImage(Image, ImageObserver) method

Syntax: public boolean prepareImage(Image image, ImageObserver observer)

Description: The prepareImage(Image, ImageObserver) method of the Component class
prepares an image to be rendered on a specified component. Java downloads the image data in another thread and then generates a suitable screen
representation of the image. This method returns a True value if the image
is already completely prepared. The image parameter indicates the image
for which you want to prepare a screen representation. The observer
parameter indicates the ImageObserver object you want Java to notify as
the image is being prepared. The ImageObserver interface defines a
method and associated constants that classes use to obtain information
asynchronously (not in concurrent time) about the status of an object. For
the most part, applications will not need to rely on this interface.

prepareImage(Image, int, int, ImageObserver) method

Syntax: public boolean prepareImage(Image image, int width, int height,
ImageObserver observer)

Component

Description: The prepareImage(Image, int, int, ImageObserver) method of the Component class instructs Java to prepare an image to be rendered at a specific
width and height on a specified component. Java downloads asynchronously the image data in another thread, and then generates an appropriately scaled screen representation of the image. Because this method is
Boolean, it returns True when the image has already been prepared. The
image parameter indicates the image for which you want Java to prepare a
screen. The width parameter indicates the width of the screen representation you want. The height parameter indicates the height of the screen
representation you want. The observer parameter indicates the
ImageObserver object you want Java to notify as the image is being
prepared.

print(Graphics) method

Syntax: public void print(Graphics g)

Description: The print(Graphics) method of the Component class prints a specified
component. The execution of the print(Graphics) method calls the paint()
method. The g parameter indicates the graphics window in which the
component is located.

```
this.print(firstButton.getGraphics());
```

printAll(Graphics) method

Syntax: public void printAll(Graphics g)

Description: The printAll(Graphics) method of the Component class prints a component
and all the subcomponents of the specified component. The g parameter
indicates the graphics window to print.

```
this.printAll(firstButton.getGraphics());
```

removeNotify() method

Syntax: public synchronized void removeNotify()

Description: The removeNotify() method of the Component class instructs Java to notify
a specified component to destroy its peer.

repaint() method

Syntax: public void repaint()

Description: The repaint() method of the Component class instructs Java to repaint a
specified component. Using this method produces a call to update the
component as soon as possible.

```
public void start() {
    textArea.appendText("Starting.\n");
    repaint();
}
```

repaint(long) method

Syntax: public void repaint(long tm)

Description: The repaint(long) method of the Component class instructs Java to repaint a specified component. Using this method produces a call to update the component with the time frame of milliseconds. The tm parameter indicates the maximum amount of time within milliseconds before the repainting takes place.

```
public void start() {
    textArea.appendText("Starting.\n");
    repaint(10); // wait 10 milliseconds, then repaint the
    ➥component
}
```

repaint(long, int, int, int, int) method

Syntax: public void repaint(int x, int y, int width, int height)

Description: The repaint(long, int, int, int, int) method of the Component class instructs Java to repaint the parts of a specified component. This method sends a call to update the component as soon as possible. The x parameter indicates the x coordinate of the component to repaint. The y parameter indicates the y coordinate of the component to repaint. The width parameter indicates the width of the component to repaint. The height parameter indicates the height of the component to repaint.

```
public void start() {
    textArea.appendText("Starting.\n");
    repaint(10, 10, 50, 50);
}
```

requestFocus() method

Syntax: public void requestFocus()

Description: The requestFocus() method of the Component class requests input focus
for a specified component. When this method is successful, Java calls the
gotFocus() method.

```
TextField myField = new TextField();
myField.requestFocus();
```

reshape(int, int, int, int) method

Syntax: public synchronized void reshape(int x, int y, int width, int height)

Description: The reshape(int, int, int, int) method of the Component class reshapes a
component to a specified bounding box. The x parameter indicates the
x coordinate, and the y parameter indicates the y component. The width
parameter indicates the width of the component, and the height parameter
indicates the height of the component.

```
myLabel.reshape(10, 10, 40, 40);
```

Component

resize(Dimension) method

Syntax: public void resize(Dimension d)

Description: The resize(Dimension) method of the Component class resizes a component to a specified dimension. The d parameter indicates the dimension you
want.

```
Dimension dim = new Dimension(width + 10, height + 10);
resize(dim);
```

resize(int, int) method

Syntax: public void resize(int width, int height)

Description: The resize(int, int) method of the Component class resizes a component
to a specified height and width. The width parameter indicates the width
of the component. The height parameter indicates the height of the
component.

```
Dimension dim = new Dimension(width + 10, height + 10);
resize(dim);
```

setBackground(Color) method

Syntax: public synchronized void setBackground(Color c)

Description: The setBackground(Color) method of the Component class sets the background color of a specified component. You use the c parameter to indicate
the color you want.

```
Color buttonColor = firstButton.getBackground();
secondButton.setBackground(buttonColor);
```

setFont(Font) method

Syntax: public synchronized void setFont(Font f)

Description: The setFont(Font) method of the Component class chooses and sets a font
for a particular component, such as the font you want to appear on buttons
or menus. The f parameter indicates the font you specify.

```
Font myFont = new Font("TimesRoman", Font.ITALIC, 24);
String myString = "Does resize work in my applet?";
g.setFont(myFont);
g.drawString(myString, 5, 5);
```

setForeground(Color) method

Syntax: public synchronized void setForeground(Color c)

Description: The setForeground(Color) method of the Component class sets the foreground color of a component. The c parameter indicates the color you
specify.

```
Color buttonColor = firstButton.getForeground();
secondButton.setForeground(buttonColor);
```

show() method

Syntax: public synchronized void show()

Component

Description: The show() method of the Component class shows a specified component on-screen.

```
selectors.add(firstButton = new Button("First"));
selectors.add(secondButton = new Button("Second"));
secondButton.show(false); // don't show this one
selectors.add(thirdButton = new Button("Third"));
```

show(boolean) method

Syntax: public void show(boolean cond)

Description: The show(boolean) method of the Component class displays the component on-screen. You use the cond parameter to indicate True to show the component on-screen and False to hide the component.

size() method

Syntax: public Dimension size()

Description: The size() method of the Component class returns the current size of a specified component.

```
Dimension dim = myFrame.size();
dim.height += 5;
dim.width += 5;
resize(dim);
```

toString() method

Syntax:　　public String toString()

Description:　The toString() method of the Component class calls a String representation of the values of a specified component.

```
System.out.println("The string representation of this button is
" +
    myButton.toString());
```

update(Graphics) method

Syntax:　　public void update(Graphics g)

Description:　The update(Graphics) method of the Component class requests that Java update a specified component. The update(Graphics) method is called in response to a call to repaint a particular component. The g parameter indicates the graphics window you want to update.

validate() method

Syntax:　　public void validate()

Description:　The validate() method of the Component class instructs Java to validate a component.

Container Class

Description: The Container class creates containers, such as panels and windows, that hold other awt containers and/or components that appear on-screen. The panel probably is the most common container. The Container class is a child of the Component class.

Methods

add(Component) method

Syntax: public synchronized Component add(Component comp)

Description: The add(Component) method of the Container class adds a specified component to the container you want. The comp parameter indicates the component you want to add.

```
buttonPanel = new Panel(); // Panel is a subclass of Container
buttonPanel.setLayout(new FlowLayout());
buttonPanel.add(okButton);
buttonPanel.add(cancelButton);
```

add(Component, int) method

Syntax: public synchronized Component add(Component comp, int pos)

Description: The add(Component, int) method of the Container class adds a specific component to a particular container in the position you specify. The comp parameter indicates the component you want to add. The pos parameter indicates the position at which you want Java to insert the component. Using 1 for the int parameter indicates to place the component at the end.

```
cbGroup = new CheckboxGroup();
cBox = new Checkbox("Check Me", cbGroup, false);
dBox = new Checkbox("No, Check ME", cbGroup, false);
fButtonPanel.add(cBox, 0);
fButtonPanel.add(dBox, 1);
```

add(String, Component) method

Syntax: public synchronized Component add(String name, Component comp)

Description: The add(String, Component) method of the Container class adds a specified component to the container you want. Java also adds the component to the layout manager of that particular container, using the name you specified. The name parameter indicates the name of the component to which you want to add another component. The comp parameter indicates the name of the component you want to add to the container.

```
buttonPanel = new Panel();
buttonPanel.setLayout(new FlowLayout());
buttonPanel.add("OKButton", okButton);
buttonPanel.add("Cancel Button", cancelButton);
```

addNotify() method

Syntax: public synchronized void addNotify()

Container

Description: The addNotify() method of the Container class instructs Java to notify a specified container to create a peer. Using this method also notifies the components within the container.

countComponents() method

Syntax: public int countComponents()

Description: The countComponents() method of the Container class returns the number of components in a specified panel.

```
System.err.println("The buttonPanel contains " +
    Integer.toString(buttonPanel.countComponents()) +
➥" components.");
```

deliverEvent(Event) method

Syntax: public void deliverEvent(Event e)

Description: The deliverEvent(Event) method of the Container class instructs Java to deliver an event to a specified component. The e parameter indicates the event you want to deliver. This method overrides the deliverEvent method in the Component class.

```
myPanel.deliverEvent(e);
```

getComponent(int) method

Syntax: public synchronized Component getComponent(int n)

Description: The getComponent(int) method of the Container class instructs Java to return the *nth* component in a specified container. The n parameter indicates the number of the component you want to get. When the nth value does not exist, this method throws an ArrayIndexOutOfBoundsException.

```
System.err.println("comp == " +
    fButtonPanel.getComponent(1).toString());
```

getComponents() method

Syntax: public synchronized Component[] getComponents()

Description: The getComponents() method of the Container class returns all the components in a specified container.

```
int x;
Component [] cArray = fButtonPanel.getComponents();
for (x = 0; x < fButtonPanel.countComponents(); ++x) {
    System.err.println("comp == " + cArray[x].toString());
}
```

getLayout() method

Syntax: public LayoutManager getLayout()

Container

Description: The getLayout() method of the Container class returns the layout manager for a specified container.

```
myLayout = buttonPanel.getLayout();
```

insets() method

Syntax: public Insets insets()

Description: The insets() method of the Container class returns the insets (the size of the border of the container) of a specified container.

```
Insets borders = myContainer.insets();
borders.top += 5;
borders.bottom += 5;
```

layout() method

Syntax: public synchronized void layout()

Description: The layout() method of the Container class instructs Java to perform a layout on a specified container.

list(PrintStream, int) method

Syntax: public void list(PrintStream out, int indent)

Description: The list(PrintStream, int) method of the Container class prints a list that begins at a specified indentation and goes to the out stream you specify. The out parameter indicates the stream name to print up to. The indent parameter indicates the indentation (or start of the list) at which you want to begin. This method overrides the list method in the Component class.

```
fButtonPanel.list(System.out, 5);
```

locate(int, int) method

Syntax: public Component locate(int x, int y)

Description: The locate(int, int) method of the Container class locates a component that contains a specified x,y position. When the component you want is not within the x,y coordinates, Java returns null. The x parameter indicates the x coordinate of the component you are trying to locate. The y parameter indicates the y coordinate of the component you are trying to locate. This method overrides the locate method in the Component class.

```
myComponent = this.locate(50, 50);
```

minimumSize() method

Syntax: public synchronized Dimension minimumSize()

Description: The minimumSize() method of the Container class returns the minimum size of a specified container. This method overrides the minimumSize method in the Component class.

Container

paintComponents(Graphics) method

Syntax: public void paintComponents(Graphics g)

Description: The paintComponents(Graphics) method of the Container class specifies the components of a container you want to paint. The g parameter indicates the graphics window in which the components and containers are located.

```
myContainer.paintComponents(myContainer.getGraphics());
```

paramString() method

Syntax: protected String paramString()

Description: The paramString() method of the Container class returns the parameter String of a specified container you specify. This method overrides the paramString method in the Component class.

```
System.out.println("The parameter string for myContainer is " +
    myContainer.paramString());
```

preferredSize() method

Syntax: public synchronized Dimension preferredSize()

Description: The preferredSize() method of the Container class returns the size you want of a specified container.

printComponents(Graphics) method

Syntax: public void printComponents(Graphics g)

Description: The printComponents(Graphics) method of the Container class prints components in from a specified container. The g parameter indicates the graphics window in which the container you specify is located.

```
myContainer.printComponents(myContainer.getGraphics());
```

remove(Components) method

Syntax: public synchronized void remove(Component comp)

Description: The remove(Components) method of the Container class removes a particular component from a specified container. The comp parameter indicates the component you want to remove.

```
myContainer.remove(firstButton);
```

removeAll() method

Syntax: public synchronized void remove(Component comp)

Description: The removeAll() method of the Container class removes all components from a specified container. The comp parameter indicates the components you want to remove.

Container

```
buttonPanel.removeAll();
```

removeNotify() method

Syntax: public synchronized void removeNotify()

Description: The removeNotify() method of the Container class instructs a specified container to remove its peer. Using this method also notifies the components in the container you specify.

setLayout(LayoutManager) method

Syntax: public void setLayout(LayoutManager mgr)

Description: The setLayout(LayoutManager) method of the Container class sets the layout manager for a specified container. The layout manager determines how sections of the screen are divided and the placement of components within those sections. The mgr parameter indicates the layout manager you specify.

```
myContainer.setLayout(new FlowLayout());
```

validate() method

Syntax: public synchronized void validate()

Description: The validate() method of the Container class instructs Java to validate a specified container and also validates all the components within that particular container.

Dialog Class

Description: The Dialog class creates dialog boxes (nonsizable and modal) that provide user information (such as warnings) and dialog boxes that accept user input, such as those boxes that contain text boxes, checkboxes, and so on. The Dialog class is a subclass of Window. The default layout for a dialog box is BorderLayout.

Constructors

Dialog(Frame, boolean) constructor

Syntax: public Dialog(Frame parent, boolean modal)

Description: The Dialog(Frame, boolean) constructor of the Dialog class constructs a dialog that initially is invisible. Java instructs a *modal dialog* (a dialog that deals with all user input until it is handled) to grab all user input. The parent parameter indicates the owner of the dialog. The modal parameter, when True, instructs the Dialog method to block input to other windows when they appear on-screen.

```
Dialog d = new Dialog(this, true); // create modal dialog

Panel buttonPanel = new Panel();
buttonPanel.setLayout(new FlowLayout());
buttonPanel.add(new Button("Yes"));
buttonPanel.add(new Button("No"));
d.add("South", buttonPanel);

d.add("Center", new Label("Are you sure you want to quit?"));
d.resize(300, 200);
d.show();
```

Dialog(Frame, String, boolean) constructor

Syntax: public Dialog(Frame parent, String title, boolean modal)

Description: The Dialog(Frame, String, boolean) constructor of the Dialog class constructs a dialog that contains a title, but initially is invisible. The parent parameter indicates the owner of the dialog. The title parameter indicates the title of the dialog box. The modal parameter indicates True (that the dialog box accepts user input); when the dialog box is on-screen, it will block input to other windows.

```
Dialog myDialog = new Dialog(this, "Are You Sure?", true);
Panel buttonPanel = new Panel();
buttonPanel.setLayout(new FlowLayout());
buttonPanel.add(new Button("Yes"));
buttonPanel.add(new Button("No"));
myDialog.add("South", buttonPanel);
myDialog.add("Center",
    new Label("Are you sure you want to quit?"));
myDialog.resize(200, 150);
myDialog.show();
```

Methods

addNotify() method

Syntax: public synchronized void addNotify()

Description: The addNotify() method of the Dialog class creates a peer for a specified dialog box. Peers enable you to change the way the frame looks while keeping the functionality of the frame the same.

getTitle() method

Syntax: public String getTitle()

Description: The getTitle() method of the Dialog class returns the title of the dialog.

```
System.err.println("The title of my dialog is " +
    myDialog.getTitle());
```

isModal() method

Syntax: public boolean isModal()

Description: The isModal() method of the Dialog class determines whether a specified
dialog box is modal (can receive user input). Because this method is
Boolean, it returns True when the dialog box is modal and False when the
dialog box is not modal.

```
if (myDialog.isModal() == true) {
    System.err.println("My dialog is modal.");
} else {
    System.err.println("My dialog is not modal.");
}
```

isResizable() method

Syntax: public boolean is Resizable()

Description: The isResizable() method of the Dialog class determines whether the user can resize a frame. Because this method is Boolean, it returns True when the user can resize the frame and False when the user cannot.

```
if (myDialog.isResizable() == true) {
    System.err.println("I can resize my dialog.");
} else {
    System.err.println("I cannot resize my dialog.");
}
```

paramString() method

Syntax: protected String paramString()

Description: The paramString() method of the Dialog class returns the parameter String of a specified dialog box. This method overrides the paramString method in the Container class.

```
class ConfirmDialog extends Dialog {

    public ConfirmDialog(Frame parentFrame, String s) {
        super(parentFrame, true);
        Panel buttonPanel = new Panel();
        buttonPanel.setLayout(new FlowLayout());
        buttonPanel.add(new Button("Yes"));
        buttonPanel.add(new Button("No"));
        add("South", buttonPanel);
        add("Center", new Label(s));
        resize(200, 150);
        setTitle("Are You Sure?");
        System.out.println("Confirm Dialog's parameter string is
        ➥" +
            super.paramString());
    }
}
```

setResizable(boolean) method

Syntax: public void setResizable(boolean resizable)

Description: The setResizable(boolean) method of the Dialog class determines whether you can resize the resizable flag. Because this method is Boolean, it returns True if the flag is resizable and False if the flag is not resizable.

```
Dialog d = new Dialog(this, true);  // create modal dialog
Panel buttonPanel = new Panel();
buttonPanel.setLayout(new FlowLayout());
buttonPanel.add(new Button("Yes"));
buttonPanel.add(new Button("No"));
d.add("South", buttonPanel);
d.add("Center", new Label("Are you sure you want to quit?"));
d.resize(200, 150);
d.setResizable(true);
d.show();
```

setTitle(String) method

Syntax: public void setTitle(String title)

Description: The setTitle(String) method of the Dialog class creates a title for a dialog box. The title parameter indicates the new title you want to give to the dialog.

```
Dialog d = new Dialog(this, true);  // create modal dialog
Panel buttonPanel = new Panel();
buttonPanel.setLayout(new FlowLayout());
buttonPanel.add(new Button("Yes"));
buttonPanel.add(new Button("No"));
d.add("South", buttonPanel);
d.add("Center", new Label("Are you sure you want to quit?"));
d.resize(200, 150);
d.setTitle("Are You Sure?");
d.show();
```

Dimension Class

Description: The Dimension class describes the height and width of a specified object.

Constructors

Dimension() constructor

Syntax: public Dimension()

Description: The Dimension() constructor of the Dimension class constructs a dimen-
                sion that has a 0 height and 0 width.

```
Dimension dim = new Dimension();
dim.width = 10;
dim.height = 20;
this.resize(dim);
```

Dimension(Dimension) constructor

Syntax: public Dimension(Dimension d)

Description: The Dimension(Dimension) constructor of the Dimension class constructs
                a dimension and initializes it to a specified value. The d parameter indi-
                cates the specified dimension for the height and width values.

```
Dimension newDim = new Dimension(oldDim); // dupl. the size of
⮕oldDim
this.resize(newDim);
```

Dimension(int, int) constructor

Syntax: public Dimension(int width, int height)

Description: The Dimension(int, int) constructor of the Dimension class constructs a
                 dimension and initializes it to a specified width and height. The width
                 parameter indicates the specified width of the dimension. The height
                 parameter indicates the specified height of the dimension.

```
Dimension dim = new Dimension(10, 20);
this.resize(dim);
```

Methods

toString() method

Syntax: public String to String()

Description: The toString() method of the Dimension class returns a String representa-
                 tion of the values of the specified dimensions.

```
System.err.println("The dimension is " +
myDim.toString());
```

Dimension

Variables

width variable

Syntax: public int width

Description: The width variable of the Dimension class specifies the width dimension of an object.

height variable

Syntax: public int height

Description: The height variable of the Dimension class specifies the height dimension of an object.

Event Class

Description: The Event class customizes the way in which your Java program handles events (or actions), such as user input or changes to the system environment. This class also contains variables that describe GUI events or actions.

Constructors

Event(Object, int, Object) constructor

Syntax: public Event(Object target, int id, Object arg)

Description: The Event(Object, int, Object) constructor of the Event class constructs an event using a specific target component (the object for which you want the action to occur), event type (type of action), and argument (the value specific to a particular event). The target parameter indicates the object for which the event is taking place. The id parameter indicates the event type. The arg parameter indicates the argument you specify.

```
Event myEvt = new Event(this, Event.KEY_RELEASE, this);
this.deliverEvent(myEvt);
```

Event(Object, long, int, int, int, int, int) constructor

Syntax: public Event(Object target, long when, int id, int x, int y, int key, int modifiers)

Event

Description: The Event(Object, long, int, int, int, int, int) constructor of the Event class constructs an event that has a specific target component (the object for which you want the action to occur), a time stamp (the time at which you want the event to take place), event type (type of action), x and y coordinates, and keyboard key. This constructor also specifies the state of the modifier keys. The target parameter indicates the object for which you want the action or event to occur. The when parameter indicates the time you want the action to occur. The id parameter indicates the type of event. The x parameter indicates the x coordinate of the event. The y parameter indicates the y coordinate of the event. The key parameter indicates the key the user presses in the keyboard event. The modifiers parameter indicates the state of the modifier keys used.

```
Event myEvt = new Event(this, 0, Event.KEY_RELEASE,
    10, 10, Event.HOME, Event.SHIFT_MASK | Event.META_MASK);
this.deliverEvent(myEvt);
```

Event(Object, long, int, int, int, int, int, Object) constructor

Syntax: (Object target, long when, int id, int x, int y, int key, int modifiers, Object arg)

Description: The Event(Object, long, int, int, int, int, int) constructor of the Event class constructs an event that has a specific target component, a time stamp, event type, x and y coordinates, and keyboard key. This constructor also specifies the state of the modifier keys and sets an argument to null. The target parameter indicates the object for which you want the action or event to occur. The when parameter indicates the time you want the action to occur. The id parameter indicates the type of event. The x parameter indicates the x coordinate of the event. The y parameter indicates the y coordinate of the event. The key parameter indicates the key the user presses in the keyboard event. The modifiers parameter indicates the modifier keys used. The arg parameter indicates the argument you specify.

```
Event myEvt = new Event(this, 0, Event.KEY_RELEASE,
    10, 10, Event.HOME, Event.SHIFT_MASK ¦ Event.META_MASK,
    this);
this.deliverEvent(myEvt);
```

Methods

controlDown() method

Syntax: public boolean controlDown()

Description: The controlDown() method of the Event class determines whether the Control key is being held down. Because this method is Boolean, it returns True when the Control key is being pressed and False when the Control key is not being pressed.

metaDown() method

Syntax: public boolean metaDown()

Description: The metaDown() method of the Event class determines whether the Meta key (the key that has the diamond symbol on it) on the Sun keyboard is being pressed. This key is the right Control key on Solaris x86 systems.

```
public boolean keyUp(Event e, int key) {
    if (key == Event.HOME && e.metaDown()) {
        System.err.println("You pressed META-HOME");
        return(true);
    } else {
        return(false);
    }
}
```

Event

paramString() method

Syntax: protected String paramString()

Description: The paramString() method of the Event class returns the parameter String
of a specified event.

```
System.err.println("The parameter string for myEvent is " +
    myEvent.paramString());
```

shiftDown() method

Syntax: public boolean shiftDown()

Description: The shiftDown() method of the Event class determines whether the Shift
key is being pressed. Because this method is Boolean, it returns True when
the Shift key is pressed and False when the Shift key is not pressed.

```
public boolean keyUp(Event e, int key) {
    if (key == Event.HOME && e.shiftDown()) {
        System.err.println("You pressed SHIFT-HOME");
        return(true);
    } else {
        return(false);
    }
}
```

toString() method

Syntax: public String toString()

Description: The toString() method of the Event class returns the String representation
                of the values of a specified event.

```
public boolean handleEvent(Event e) {
        System.err.println("Event received: " e.toString());
        return(super.handleEvent(e));
}
```

translate(int, int) method

Syntax: public void translate(int x, int y)

Description: The translate(int, int) method of the Event class translates a relative event
                or action to a specified component. Java translates the coordinates of the
                action so that the component can understand. In the case of an expose
                event, this method also may involve translating a region as well as coordi-
                nates. The x parameter indicates the x coordinate of the action. The
                y parameter indicates the y coordinate of the action.

```
public boolean handleEvent(Event e) {
    switch(e.id) {

    case Event.WINDOW_EXPOSE:
            e.translate(10, 10);
            break;
```

Event

Variables

ACTION EVENT variable

Syntax: public final static int ACTION_EVENT

Description: The ACTION EVENT variable of the Event class specifies the action event you want to take place.

ALT MASK variable

Syntax: public final static int ALT_MASK

Description: The ALT MASK variable of the Event class indicates the action of the Alt key being pressed. The Alt key is a modifier key when pressed in conjunction with a second key.

arg variable

Syntax: public Object arg

Description: The arg variable of the Event class indicates a value that is specific to the action taking place.

CTRL MASK variable

Syntax: public final static int CTRL_MASK

Description: The CTRL MASK variable of the Event class indicates the action of the Control key being pressed. The Control key is a modifier key when pressed in conjunction with a second key.

DOWN variable

Syntax: public final static int DOWN

Description: The DOWN variable of the Event class indicates the action of the down arrow key being pressed.

END variable

Syntax: public final static int END

Description: The END variable of the Event class indicates the action of the END key being pressed.

ESC variable

Syntax: public final static int ESC

Description: The ESC variable of the Event class indicates the action of the ESC key being pressed.

evt variable

Syntax: public Event evt

Description: The evt variable of the Event class indicates the next event. You use this variable when placing events in a linked list.

F1 variable

Syntax: public final static int F1

Description: The F1 variable of the Event class indicates the action of the F1 function key being pressed.

F2 variable

Syntax: public final static int F2

Description: The F2 variable of the Event class indicates the action of the F2 function key being pressed.

F3 variable

Syntax: public final static int F3

Description: The F3 variable of the Event class indicates the action of the F3 function key being pressed.

F4 variable

Syntax: public final static int F4

Description: The F4 variable of the Event class indicates the action of the F4 function key being pressed.

F5 variable

Syntax: public final static int F5

Description: The F5 variable of the Event class indicates the action of the F5 function key being pressed.

F6 variable

Syntax: public final static int F6

Description: The F6 variable of the Event class indicates the action of the F6 function key being pressed.

F7 variable

Syntax: public final static int F7

Description: The F7 variable of the Event class indicates the action of the F7 function key being pressed.

Event

F8 variable

Syntax:　　public final static int F8

Description:　The F8 variable of the Event class indicates the action of the F8 function key being pressed.

F9 variable

Syntax:　　public final static int F9

Description:　The F9 variable of the Event class indicates the action of the F9 function key being pressed.

F10 variable

Syntax:　　public final static int F10

Description:　The F10 variable of the Event class indicates the action of the F10 function key being pressed.

F11 variable

Syntax:　　public final static int F11

Description:　The F11 variable of the Event class indicates the action of the F11 function key being pressed.

F12 variable

Syntax: public final static int F12

Description: The F12 variable of the Event class indicates the action of the F12 function key being pressed.

GOT FOCUS variable

Syntax: public final static int GOT_FOCUS

Description: The GOT FOCUS variable of the Event class indicates that a component now has the focus.

HOME variable

Syntax: public final static int HOME

Description: The HOME variable of the Event class indicates that the Home key is being pressed.

id variable

Syntax: public int id

Description: The id variable of the Event class specifies the type of event you want to take place.

Event

key variable

Syntax: public int key

Description: The key variable of the Event class indicates the key being pressed in a keyboard event.

KEY ACTION variable

Syntax: public final static int KEY_ACTION

Description: The KEY ACTION variable of the Event class indicates the key field containing one of the constant's identifiers defined in the Event class (Event.PGUP, Event.PGDN, etc.), which is a key action keyboard event.

KEY ACTION RELEASE variable

Syntax: public final static int KEY_ACTION_RELEASE

Description: The KEY ACTION RELEASE variable of the Event class indicates the release of a key (a key action keyboard event).

KEY PRESS variable

Syntax: public final static int KEY_PRESS

Description: The KEY PRESS variable of the Event class indicates that a key on the keyboard is being pressed. The key field of the Event will contain the Unicode character code for the character

KEY RELEASE variable

Syntax: public final static int KEY_RELEASE

Description: The KEY RELEASE variable of the Event class indicates that a keyboard key has been released.

LEFT variable

Syntax: public final static int LEFT

Description: The LEFT variable of the Event class indicates that the left arrow key is being pressed.

LIST DESELECT variable

Syntax: public final static int LIST_DESELECT

Description: The LIST DESELECT variable of the Event class indicates that an option has been deselected from a list.

Event

LIST SELECT variable

Syntax:　　　public final static int LIST_SELECT

Description:　The LIST SELECT variable of the Event class indicates that a list option has been selected.

LOAD FILE variable

Syntax:　　　public final static int LOAD_FILE

Description:　The LOAD FILE variable of the Event class indicates the action of a file being loaded.

LOST FOCUS variable

Syntax:　　　public final static int LOST_FOCUS

Description:　The LOST FOCUS variable of the Event class indicates that a component no longer has the focus.

META MASK variable

Syntax:　　　public final static int META_MASK

Description:　The META MASK variable of the Event class indicates the action of the Meta key being pressed. The Meta key contains a diamond shape and is found on the Sun keyboard. It is the right Control key on x86 system keyboards. The Meta key is a modifier key when pressed in conjunction with a second key.

modifiers variable

Syntax: public int modifiers

Description: The modifiers variable of the Event class indicates whether a modifier key is being pressed. A *modifier key* is one that, when pressed in conjunction with another key, changes the action of the second key, such as the Control key and the Alt key.

MOUSE DOWN variable

Syntax: public final static int MOUSE_DOWN

Description: The MOUSE DOWN variable of the Event class indicates that the mouse button is being pressed.

MOUSE DRAG variable

Syntax: public final static int MOUSE_DRAG

Description: The MOUSE DRAG variable of the Event class indicates the mouse drag action.

Event

MOUSE ENTER variable

Syntax: public final static int MOUSE_ENTER

Description: The MOUSE ENTER variable of the Event class indicates when the mouse pointer enters an applet.

MOUSE EXIT variable

Syntax: public final static int MOUSE_EXIT

Description: The MOUSE EXIT variable of the Event class indicates when the mouse pointer has exited a frame.

MOUSE MOVE variable

Syntax: public final static int MOUSE_MOVE

Description: The MOUSE MOVE variable of the Event class indicates that the mouse pointer has moved. This does not include a mouse button being pressed.

MOUSE UP variable

Syntax: public final static int MOUSE_UP

Description: The MOUSE UP variable of the Event class indicates the action of the mouse button being released.

PGDN variable

Syntax: public final static int PGDN

Description: The PGDN variable of the Event class indicates that the Page Down key is being pressed.

PGUP variable

Syntax: public final static int PGUP

Description: The PGUP variable of the Event class indicates that the Page Up key is being pressed.

RIGHT variable

Syntax: public final static int RIGHT

Description: The RIGHT variable of the Event class indicates that the right arrow key has been pressed.

SAVE FILE variable

Syntax: public final static int SAVE_FILE

Description: The SAVE FILE variable of the Event class indicates that a file has been saved.

Event

SCROLL ABSOLUTE variable

Syntax: public final static int SCROLL_ABSOLUTE

Description: The SCROLL ABSOLUTE variable of the Event class indicates the absolute location of an event designated by use of the "tab" in the scrollbar. This does not apply to using the up/down arrows or the page up/down functionality.

SCROLL LINE DOWN variable

Syntax: public final static int SCROLL_LINE_DOWN

Description: The SCROLL LINE DOWN variable of the Event class indicates the action of scrolling down one line.

SCROLL LINE UP variable

Syntax: public final static int SCROLL_LINE_UP

Description: The SCROLL LINE UP variable of the Event class indicates that the page has scrolled up one line.

SCROLL PAGE DOWN variable

Syntax: public final static int SCROLL_PAGE_DOWN

Description: The SCROLL PAGE DOWN variable of the Event class indicates that the screen has scrolled down one page.

SCROLL PAGE UP variable

Syntax: public final static int SCROLL_PAGE_UP

Description: The SCROLL PAGE UP variable of the Event class indicates that the screen has scrolled up one page.

SHIFT MASK variable

Syntax: public final static int SHIFT_MASK

Description: The SHIFT MASK variable of the Event class indicates that the Shift key has been pressed.

target variable

Syntax: public Object target

Description: The target variable of the Event class specifies the component for which you want the event or action to occur.

UP variable

Syntax: public final static int UP

Description: The UP variable of the Event class indicates that the up arrow key has been pressed.

when variable

Syntax: public long when

Description: The when variable of the Event class indicates the time when the event or action took place.

WINDOW DEICONIFY variable

Syntax: public final static int WINDOW_DEICONIFY

Description: The WINDOW DEICONIFY variable of the Event class indicates the action of a window being maximized (or de-iconified) from an icon.

WINDOW DESTROY variable

Syntax: public final static int WINDOW_DESTROY

Description: The WINDOW DESTROY variable of the Event class indicates that a window has been closed (or destroyed).

WINDOW EXPOSE variable

Syntax: public final static int WINDOW_EXPOSE

Description: The WINDOW EXPOSE variable of the Event class indicates that a window has been made active (or exposed).

WINDOW ICONIFY variable

Syntax: public final static int WINDOW_ICONIFY

Description: The WINDOW ICONIFY variable of the Event class indicates the action of a window being minimized (or iconified).

WINDOW MOVED variable

Syntax: public final static int WINDOW_MOVED

Description: The WINDOW MOVED variable of the Event class indicates that a window has been moved.

x variable

Syntax: public int x

Description: The x variable of the Event class specifies the x coordinate of the event or action you want to take place.

Event

y variable

Syntax: public int y

Description: The y variable of the Event class specifies the y coordinate of the event or action you want to take place.

FileDialog Class

Description: The FileDialog class displays a file selection dialog box (File Open and File Save). This type of dialog box is modal (accepts user input), and until the user chooses a file, it blocks the calling thread when you use the show() method to display it.

Constructors

FileDialog(Frame, String) constructor

Syntax: public FileDialog(Frame parent, String title)

Description: The FileDialog(Frame, String) constructor of the FileDialog class creates a dialog box that enables the user to load (or open) a file. The parent parameter indicates the owner of the dialog box. The title parameter indicates the title of the dialog box you are creating.

```
FileDialog fd = new FileDialog(this, "Open a file");
fd.show();
```

FileDialog(Frame, String, int) constructor

Syntax: public FileDialog(Frame parent, String title, int mode)

Description: The FileDialog(Frame, String, int) constructor of the FileDialog class creates a file dialog box that contains a specified title and a particular mode (File Open or File Save). The parent parameter indicates the owner of the

FileDialog

dialog box. The title parameter indicates the title of the dialog box. The mode parameter indicates the mode of the dialog box (Open or Save).

```
FileDialog fd = new FileDialog(this, "Open a file",
FileDialog.LOAD);
fd.setFile("test.html");
fd.show();
```

Methods

addNotify() method

Syntax: public synchronized void addNotify()

Description: The addNotify() method of the FileDialog class creates a peer of a specified frame. Creating a peer enables you to modify the appearance of the file dialog box while maintaining the functionality of the frame.

getDirectory() method

Syntax: public String getDirectory()

Description: The getDirectory method of the FileDialog class returns the directory of the dialog box.

```
FileDialog fd = new FileDialog(this, "Open a file");
fd.show();
String fileName = fd.getFile();
System.out.println("You selected the file " + fileName +
    "in the directory " + fd.getDirectory());
```

getFile() method

Syntax: public String getFile()

Description: The getFile() method of the FileDialog class returns the file of the dialog box you specify.

```
FileDialog fd = new FileDialog(this, "Open a file");
fd.show();
String fileName = fd.getFile();
System.out.println("You selected the file " + fileName);
```

getFilenameFilter() method

Syntax: public FilenameFilter getFilenameFilter()

Description: The getFilenameFilter() method of the FileDialog class returns the *filter* (the command that reads the standard input) of the specified dialog box.

```
FileDialog fd = new FileDialog(this, "Open a file");
FilenameFilter filter = fd.getFilenameFilter();
fd.show();
```

getMode() method

Syntax: public int getMode()

Description: The getMode() method of the FileDialog class determines the operational
state of the specified dialog box.

```
FileDialog fd = new FileDialog(this, "Open a file");
if (fd.getMode() == FileDialog.LOAD) {
    System.err.println("LOADing");
} else {
    System.err.println("SAVEing");
}
fd.show();
```

paramString() method

Syntax: protected String paramString()

Description: The paramString() method of the FileDialog class returns the parameter
String of the specified file dialog box. This method overrides the
paramString method in the Dialog class.

setDirectory(String) method

Syntax: public void setDirectory(String dir)

Description: The setDirectory(String) method of the FileDialog class sets a specific
directory for the specified dialog box. The dir parameter indicates the
directory you want to set.

```
FileDialog fd = new FileDialog(this, "Open a file");
fd.setDirectory("c:\\src");
fd.show();
```

setFile(String) method

Syntax: public void setFile(String file)

Description: The setFile(String) method of the FileDialog class sets the file for a
particular dialog box to a specified file. The file you set becomes the
default file if you set it before the dialog box appears. The file parameter
indicates the file you want to set.

```
FileDialog fd = new FileDialog(this, "Open a file");
fd.setFile("test.html");
fd.show();
```

setFilenameFilter(FilenameFilter) method

Syntax: public void setFilenameFilter(FilenameFilter filter)

Description: The setFilenameFilter() method of the FileDialog class sets the filter
(the command that reads the standard input) of the specified dialog box.
The filter parameter indicates the filter you want to set.

```
FileDialog fd = new FileDialog(this, "Open a file");
fd.setFile("test.html");
fd.setFilenameFilter(new JavaFilter());
fd.show();
```

FileDialog

Variables

LOAD variable

Syntax: public final static int LOAD

Description: The LOAD method specifies that a dialog box be capable of loading (opening) a file.

SAVE variable

Syntax: public final static int SAVE

Description: The SAVE variable of the FileDialog class indicates that the user has chosen the Save option in a modal dialog box.

FlowLayout Class

Description: The FlowLayout class arranges on a panel components (buttons) in rows, from left to right. When no more buttons fit on a row, this class wraps the buttons to the next line. By default, the rows of buttons are centered; however, you can use other methods in this class to specify right alignment and left alignment. You also can add space between rows of components. This is done by setting horizontal and vertical gap values.

Constructors

FlowLayout() constructor

Syntax: public FlowLayout()

Description: The FlowLayout() constructor of the FlowLayout class creates a new flow layout that is centered.

```
myPanel.setLayout(new FlowLayout()); // center alignment
```

FlowLayout(int) constructor

Syntax: public FlowLayout(int align)

Description: The FlowLayout(int) constructor of the FlowLayout class creates a new flow layout, using a specified alignment. The align parameter indicates the alignment value you want to use.

```
myPanel.setLayout(new FlowLayout(FlowLayout.RIGHT)); //
align to the right
```

FlowLayout(int, int, int) constructor

Syntax: public FlowLayout(int align, int hgap, int vgap)

Description: The FlowLayout(int, int, int) constructor of the FlowLayout class creates a
new flow layout that has specified alignments and gap values. The align
parameter indicates the type of alignment you want to use (right, left, or
centered). The hgap parameter indicates the horizontal gap you want
between components. The vgap parameter indicates the gap you want
between rows. The horizontal and vertical gap values are in pixels. By
default, the values of the horizontal and vertical gaps are three pixels.

```
myPanel.setLayout(new FlowLayout(FlowLayout.LEFT, 10,
10));
```

Methods

addLayoutComponent(String, Component) method

Syntax: public void addLayoutComponent(String name, Component comp)

Description: The addLayoutComponent(String, Component) method of the FlowLayout
class adds a specified component to a particular layout. The name parameter indicates the name of the component. The comp parameter indicates
the name of the specific component you want to add. This method is for
internal use by the layout manager and should not be called by the application or applet.

layoutContainer(Container) method

Syntax: public void layoutContainer(Container target)

Description: The layoutContainer(Container) method of the FlowLayout class lays out a
container. This method reshapes the components within the target container
so the constraints of the BorderLayout object are satisfied. The target
parameter indicates the container in which you want to lay out the component. This method is called by the system and should not be called by the
application or applet.

minimumLayoutSize(Container) method

Syntax: public Dimension minimumLayoutSize(Container target)

Description: The minimumLayoutSize(Container) method of the FlowLayout class
returns the minimum dimensions required to lay out a specified component
in a particular target container. The parameter indicates the container in
which you want to lay out the component. This method is called by the
system and should not be called by the application or applet.

preferredLayoutSize(Container) method

Syntax: public Dimension preferredLayoutSize(Container target)

Description: The preferredLayoutSize(Container) method of the FlowLayout class
returns the dimensions you want for a particular layout. The dimensions
are based on the components in the specified target container. The target
parameter indicates the component you want to lay out.

removeLayoutComponent(Component) method

Syntax: public void removeLayoutComponent(Component comp)

Description: The removeLayoutComponent(Component) method of the FlowLayout class removes a specified component (button) from a particular layout. The comp parameter indicates the component you want to remove.

toString() method

Syntax: public String toString()

Description: The toString() method of the FlowLayout class returns a String representation of the values of the flow layout you specify.

```
System.err.println("The layout for the panel is " +
    myPanel.getLayout().toString());
```

Variables

CENTER variable

Syntax: public final static int CENTER

Description: The CENTER variable of the FlowLayout class center-aligns the row you specify.

LEFT variable

Syntax: public final static int LEFT

Description: The LEFT variable of the FlowLayout class left-aligns the row you specify.

RIGHT variable

Syntax: public final static int RIGHT

Description: The RIGHT variable of the FlowLayout class right-aligns the row you specify.

Font Class

Description: The Font class creates font objects that represent an individual font, which includes the name of the font, the format (bold/italic), and the size of the font. You can specify plain or roman text, italic text, bold text, and bold italic. Java provides platform-independent standard names for five fonts that usually are available on any platform: Helvetica, TimesRoman, Courier, Dialog, and DialogInput. Java also provides the ZapfDingbat font; however, this font usually is not available on Unix platforms running the X Window System.

Constructors

Font(String, int, int) constructor

Syntax: public Font(String name, int style, int size)

Description: The Font(String, int, int) constructor of the Font class creates a new font for which you specify a name, style, and point size. The name parameter indicates the name of the font. The style parameter indicates the typestyles applied to the font. The size parameter indicates the point size of the font to be used.

```
Font myFont = new Font("TimesRoman", Font.ITALIC, 24);

String myString = "This string should be in Times Italic, 24
➥Point.";

g.setFont(myFont);
g.drawString(myString, 5, height + 5);
```

Methods

equals(Object) method

Syntax: public boolean equals(Object obj)

Description: The equals(Object) method compares one object to another. The obj
parameter indicates the object with which you are comparing. Because this
method is Boolean, it returns True when the two specified objects are the
same and False when they are not the same. The equals(Object) method
overrides the equals() method in the Object class.

```
Font firstFont = new Font("TimesRoman", Font.ITALIC, 24);
Font secondFont = new Font("TimesRoman", Font.PLAIN, 12);
Font thirdFont = new Font("Helvetica", Font.PLAIN, 12);
Font fourthFont = new Font("TimesRoman", Font.ITALIC, 24);
if (firstFont.equals(secondFont)) {
    System.err.println("firstFont == secondFont");
}
if (secondFont.equals(thirdFont)) {
    System.err.println("secondFont == thirdFont");
}
if (firstFont.equals(fourthFont)) {
    System.err.println("firstFont == fourthFont");
}
```

getFamily() method

Syntax: public String getFamily()

Description: The getFamily() method of the Font class returns the platform-specific
name of a specified font. The corresponding X font for the Java

Font

TimesRoman font, for example, is adobe-times. To find the logical name of the font, use the getName() method of the Font class.

```
Font firstFont = new Font("TimesRoman", Font.ITALIC, 24);

System.err.println("The font's family is " +
    firstFont.getFamily());
```

getFont(String) method

Syntax: public static Font getFont(String nm)

Description: The getFont(String) method of the Font class returns a font from the system properties list. The system properties list contains named resource values for specified applications. The nm parameter indicates the name of the property.

```
Font firstFont = Font.getFont("helvetica-italic-24");
String myString = "Draw This String";
g.setFont(firstFont);

g.drawString(myString, 25, height + 25);
```

getFont(String, Font) method

Syntax: public static Font getFont(String nm, Font font)

Description: The getFont(String, Font) method of the Font class returns a specified font from the system properties list. The system properties list contains named resource values for specified applications. The nm parameter indicates the name of the property. The font parameter indicates the name of the font you want to get.

```
Font firstFont = new Font("TimesRoman", Font.ITALIC, 24);
Font secondFont = Font.getFont("helvetica-italic-24",
➥firstFont);

String myString = "Draw This String";
g.setFont(secondFont);
g.drawString(myString, 25, height + 25);
```

getName() method

Syntax: public String getName()

Description: The getName() method of the Font class returns the logical name of
the font.

```
Font firstFont = new Font("TimesRoman", Font.ITALIC, 24);
System.err.println("Font name is " + firstFont.getName());
```

getSize() method

Syntax: public int getSize()

Description: The getSize() method of the Font class returns the point size of a particular
font.

```
Font firstFont = new Font("TimesRoman", Font.ITALIC, 24);
// want secondFont to be same size as firstFont
Font secondFont = new Font("Helvetica", Font.ITALIC,
    firstFont.getSize());
```

getStyle() method

Syntax: public int getStyle()

Description: The getStyle() method of the Font class returns the specified font style,
                 such as plain, bold, and italic.

```
Font firstFont = new Font("TimesRoman", Font.ITALIC, 24);
// want secondFont to be same style and size as firstFont
Font secondFont = new Font("Helvetica", firstFont.getStyle(),
    firstFont.getSize());
```

hashCode() method

Syntax: public int hashCode()

Description: The hashCode() method of the Font class returns the hash code for a
                 specified. Hash codes are used for storing objects in hash tables. The
                 hashCode() method of the Color class returns the hash code for a specified
                 object. This method is used by the java.util.Hashtable class and is not
                 typically called in an applet or application.

isBold() method

Syntax: public boolean isBold()

Description: The isBold() method of the Font class determines whether the specified
                 font is bold. Because this method is Boolean, it returns True when the font
                 is bold and False when the font is not bold.

```
Font secondFont = new Font("Helvetica", firstFont.getStyle(),
    firstFont.getSize());
if (secondFont.isBold()) {
    System.out.println("secondFont is BOLD");
}
```

isItalic() method

Syntax: public boolean isItalic()

Description: The isItalic() method of the Font class determines whether the specified font is italic. Because this method is Boolean, it returns True when the font is italic and False when the font is not italic.

```
Font secondFont = new Font("Helvetica", firstFont.getStyle(),
    firstFont.getSize());
if (secondFont.isItalic()) {
    System.out.println("secondFont is ITALIC");
}
```

isPlain() method

Syntax: public boolean isPlain()

Description: The isPlain() method of the Font class determines whether the specified font is plain (roman). Because this method is Boolean, it returns True when the font is plain and False when the font contains other formatting, such as bold or italic.

```
Font secondFont = new Font("Helvetica", firstFont.getStyle(),
    firstFont.getSize());
if (secondFont.isPlain()) {
    System.out.println("secondFont is PLAIN");
}
```

toString() method

Syntax: public String toString()

Description: The toString() method of the Font class converts an object to a String
representation.

```
System.out.println("firstFont is " +
➥firstFont.toString());
```

Variables

BOLD variable

Syntax: public final static int BOLD

Description: The BOLD variable of the Font class indicates that the font is bold.

ITALIC variable

Syntax: public final static int ITALIC

Description: The ITALIC variable of the Font class indicates that the font is italic.

name variable

Syntax: protected String name

Description: The name variable of the Font class indicates the logical name of the specified font.

PLAIN variable

Syntax: public final static int PLAIN

Description: The PLAIN variable of the Font class indicates that the font is plain (or roman), with no other formatting applied.

size variable

Syntax: protected int size

Description: The size variable of the Font class indicates the point size of the font.

style variable

Syntax: protected int style

Description: The style variable of the Font class indicates the style of the font. This variable gives you the sum of the constants—PLAIN, BOLD, or ITALIC.

Font

FontMetrics Class

Description: The FontMetrics class is a utility class for obtaining information about fonts, such as the length (in pixels) of a string or how tall the letters of a given font will be onscreen. This class is useful for scaling a window to properly display a label.

Constructors

FontMetrics(Font) constructor

Syntax: protected FontMetrics(Font font)

Description: The FontMetrics(Font) constructor of the FontMetrics class creates a new FontMetrics object with a predetermined font. The font parameter indicates the font you specify.

```
public void paint(Graphics g) {
    Font myFont = new Font("TimesRoman", Font.ITALIC, 24);
    FontMetrics myMetrics = g.getFontMetrics(myFont);
    // ...
}
```

Methods

bytesWidth(byte[], int, int) method

Syntax: public int bytesWidth(byte data[], int off, int len)

Description: The bytesWidth(byte[], int, int) method of the FontMetrics class returns the width of a a specified array of bytes in a particular font. The data parameter indicates the data you want to check. The off parameter indicates the start offset of the data you want to check. The len parameter indicates the maximum number of bytes you want to check.

```
Font myFont = new Font("TimesRoman", Font.ITALIC, 24);

FontMetrics myMetrics = g.getFontMetrics(myFont);
byte [] byteArray = new byte[3];
byteArray[0] = 'A';
byteArray[1] = 'b';
byteArray[2] = 'C';
System.err.println("byteArray is " +
    Integer.toString(myMetrics.bytesWidth(byteArray, 0, 3)) +
    " units wide.");
```

charWidth(char) method

Syntax: public int charWidth(char ch)

Description: The charWidth(char) method of the FontMetrics class returns the width of a specified character in a particular font. The ch parameter indicates the font you specify.

```
Font myFont = new Font("Helvetica", Font.ITALIC, 24);

FontMetrics myMetrics = g.getFontMetrics(myFont);
System.err.println("The letter 'I' is " +
    Integer.toString(myMetrics.charWidth('I')) +
    " units wide.");
System.err.println("The letter 'M' is " +
    Integer.toString(myMetrics.charWidth('M')) +
    " units wide.");
```

FontMetrics

charWidth(int) method

Syntax: public int charWidth(int ch)

Description: The charWidth(int) method of the FontMetrics class returns the width of a specified character in a particular font. The int parameter indicates the width you specify.

```
Font myFont = new Font("Helvetica", Font.ITALIC, 24);

FontMetrics myMetrics = g.getFontMetrics(myFont);
System.err.println("Character 150 is " +
    Integer.toString(myMetrics.charWidth(150)) +
    " units wide.");
System.err.println("Character 170 is " +
    Integer.toString(myMetrics.charWidth(170)) +
    " units wide.");
```

charsWidth(char[], int, int) method

Syntax: public int charsWidth(char data[], int off, int len)

Description: The charsWidth(char[], int, int) method of the FontMetrics class returns the width of a specified character array in a particular font. The data parameter indicates the data you want to check. The off parameter indicates the start offset of the data you want to check. The len parameter indicates the maximum number of bytes you want to check.

```
Font myFont = new Font("Helvetica", Font.ITALIC, 24);

FontMetrics myMetrics = g.getFontMetrics(myFont);
char[] charArr = new char[3];
charArr[0] = 'A';
charArr[1] = 'b';
charArr[2] = 'C';
```

```
System.err.println("charArr is " +
    Integer.toString(myMetrics.charsWidth(charArr, 0, 3)) +
    " units wide.");
```

getAscent() method

Syntax: public int getAscent()

Description: The getAscent() method of the FontMetrics class determines the *ascent* of
a font, which is the distance from the baseline of the text to the top of a
given character.

```
Font myFont = new Font("Helvetica", Font.ITALIC, 24);

FontMetrics myMetrics = g.getFontMetrics(myFont);

System.out.println("The ascent for " +
    myMetrics.getFont().toString() + " is " +
    Integer.toString(myMetrics.getAscent()));
```

getDescent() method

Syntax: public int getDescent()

Description: The getDescent() method of the FontMetrics class returns the *descent* of
the font, which is the distance from the baseline of the text line to the
bottom of a given character.

FontMetrics

```
Font myFont = new Font("Helvetica", Font.ITALIC, 24);

FontMetrics myMetrics = g.getFontMetrics(myFont);

System.out.println("The descent for " +
    myMetrics.getFont().toString() + " is " +
    Integer.toString(myMetrics.getDescent()));
```

getFont() method

Syntax: public Font getFont()

Description: The getFont() method of the FontMetrics class returns the font you specify.

```
Font myFont = new Font("Helvetica", Font.ITALIC, 24);

FontMetrics myMetrics = g.getFontMetrics(myFont);

System.out.println("The ascent for " +
    myMetrics.getFont().toString() + " is " +
    Integer.toString(myMetrics.getAscent()));
```

getHeight() method

Syntax: public int getHeight()

Description: The getHeight() method of the Font class returns the total height of a
                 specified font. The height of a font consists of the distance from the top of
                 the ascender to the bottom of the descender.

```
Font myFont = new Font("Helvetica", Font.ITALIC, 24);

FontMetrics myMetrics = g.getFontMetrics(myFont);
int height = myMetrics.getHeight();
```

getLeading() method

Syntax: public int getLeading()

Description: The getLeading() method of the FontMetrics class returns the standard
                leading (line space) for a specified font. The standard lead is the logical
                amount of space you want to reserve between the descent of one line of
                text and the ascent of the next line of text. Java calculates the height metric
                to include this extra space.

```
Font myFont = new Font("Helvetica", Font.ITALIC, 24);

FontMetrics myMetrics = g.getFontMetrics(myFont);

System.out.println("The leading for " +
    myMetrics.getFont().toString() + " is " +
    Integer.toString(myMetrics.getLeading()));
```

FontMetrics

getMaxAdvance() method

Syntax: public int getMaxAdvance()

Description: The getMaxAdvance() method of the FontMetrics class returns the maxi-
                mum advance width of any character in a specified font. This method
                returns −1 when the max advance is unknown.

```
Font myFont = new Font("Helvetica", Font.ITALIC, 24);

FontMetrics myMetrics = g.getFontMetrics(myFont);

System.out.println("The maximum advance for " +
    myMetrics.getFont().toString() + " is " +
    Integer.toString(myMetrics.getMaxAdvance()));
```

getMaxAscent() method

Syntax: public int getMaxAscent()

Description: The getMaxAscent() method of the FontMetrics class returns the maximum ascent of all characters. Using this method ensures that characters will not ascend above the baseline of the metric you specify.

```
Font myFont = new Font("Helvetica", Font.ITALIC, 24);

FontMetrics myMetrics = g.getFontMetrics(myFont);

System.out.println("The maximum ascent for " +
    myMetrics.getFont().toString() + " is " +
    Integer.toString(myMetrics.getMaxAscent()));
```

getMaxDescent() method

Syntax: public int getMaxDescent()

Description: The getMaxDescent() method of the FontMetric class returns the maximum descent of all characters. Using this method ensures that characters will not descend below the baseline of the metric you specify.

```
Font myFont = new Font("Helvetica", Font.ITALIC, 24);

FontMetrics myMetrics = g.getFontMetrics(myFont);

System.out.println("The maximum descent for " +
    myMetrics.getFont().toString() + " is " +
    Integer.toString(myMetrics.getMaxDescent()));
```

getWidths() method

Syntax: public int[] getWidths()

Description: The getWidths() method of the FontMetrics class returns the width of the
                 first 256 characters in a specified font.

```
Font myFont = new Font("Helvetica", Font.ITALIC, 24);

FontMetrics myMetrics = g.getFontMetrics(myFont);

int [] intArray = myMetrics.getWidths();
System.out.println("Character 150 is " +
    Integer.toString(intArray[150]) +
    " units wide.");
System.out.println("Character 170 is " +
    Integer.toString(intArray[170]) +
    " units wide.");
```

FontMetrics

stringWidth(String) method

Syntax: public int stringWidth(String str)

Description: The stringWidth(String) method of the FontMetrics class returns the width of a specified string of a particular font. The str parameter indicates the string you are querying.

```
Font myFont = new Font("Helvetica", Font.ITALIC, 24);

FontMetrics myMetrics = g.getFontMetrics(myFont);

String myString = "Draw This String";
int height = myMetrics.getHeight();
int width = myMetrics.stringWidth(myString);
```

toString() method

Syntax: public String toString()

Description: The toString() method of the FontMetrics class returns the String representation of the values of the FontMetric you specify.

```
Font myFont = new Font("Helvetica", Font.ITALIC, 24);

FontMetrics myMetrics = g.getFontMetrics(myFont);
System.out.println("myMetrics are " + myMetrics.toString());
```

Variables

font variable

Syntax: protected Font font

Description: The font variable of the FontMetrics class returns the actual font.

Frame Class

Description: The Frame class, which is a subclass of the Window class, creates independent, functional windows that contain menu bars. Because frames are
containers, you can add components to them.

Constructors

Frame() constructor

Syntax: public Frame()

Description: The Frame() constructor of the Frame class creates a frame that initially
does not appear on-screen.

```
Frame myFrame = new Frame();
```

Frame(String) constructor

Syntax: public Frame(String title)

Description: The Frame(String) constructor of the Frame class creates a new frame that
initially is invisible. This method also adds a title to that frame. The title
parameter indicates the title you want to assign to the frame.

```
Frame myFrame = new Frame("My Frame Title");
```

Frame

Methods

addNotify() method

Syntax: public synchronized void addNotify()

Description: The addNotify() method of the Frame class creates a peer of a specified frame. Creating a peer enables you to modify the appearance of the frame without changing its original functionality.

dispose() method

Syntax: public synchronized void dispose()

Description: The dispose() method of the Frame class disposes a frame. You must call this method in order to release the resources used for that particular frame.

```
Frame myFrame = new Frame();
// ...
myFrame.dispose();
```

getCursorType() method

Syntax: public int getCursorType()

Description: The getCursorType() method of the Frame class returns the cursor type.

```
Frame myFrame = new Frame();
myFrame.show();
int cursorType = myFrame.getCursorType();
switch (cursorType) {

case Frame.CROSSHAIR_CURSOR:
    System.out.println("Cursor: Crosshair");
    break;

case Frame.DEFAULT_CURSOR:
    System.out.println("Cursor: Default");
    break;

case Frame.E_RESIZE_CURSOR:
    System.out.println("Cursor: East Resize");
    break;

default:
    System.out.println("Other");
    break;
}
```

getIconImage() method

Syntax: public Image getIconImage()

Description: The getIconImage() method of the Frame class returns the icon image for a specified frame.

```
Image iconImage = myframe.getIconImage();
```

Frame

getMenuBar() method

Syntax: public MenuBar getMenuBar()

Description: The getMenuBar() method of the Frame class returns the menu bar for a specified frame.

```
MenuBar menuBar = myFrame.getMenuBar();
```

getTitle() method

Syntax: public String getTitle()

Description: The getTitle() method of the Frame class returns the title of a specified frame.

```
Frame myFrame = new Frame("My Title");
System.out.println("The title is:  " + myFrame.getTitle());
```

isResizable() method

Syntax: public boolean isResizable()

Description: The isResizable() method of the Frame class determines whether a user can resize a frame. Because this method is Boolean, it returns True when the user can resize the frame and False when the user cannot.

```
if (myFrame.isResizable()) {
    System.out.println("myFrame is resizable.");
} else {
    System.out.println("myFrame is not resizable.");
}
```

paramString() method

Syntax: protected String paramString()

Description: The paramString() method of the Frame class returns the parameter string of the frame.

```
System.out.println("myFrame's parameter string is " +
        myFrame.paramString());
```

remove(MenuComponent) method

Syntax: public synchronized void remove(MenuComponent m)

Description: The remove(MenuComponent) method of the Frame class removes a menu bar from a particular frame. The m parameter indicates the menu bar component you want to remove.

```
MenuBar = myFrame.getMenuBar();
myFrame.remove(menuBar);
```

Frame

setIconImage(Image) method

Syntax: public void setIconImage(Image image)

Description: The setIconImage(Image) method of the Frame class assigns an image to
                 appear when you iconize (minimize) a frame. The image parameter indi-
                 cates the icon you want to appear when the window is minimized.

```
myFrame.setIconImage(myImage);
```

setMenuBar(MenuBar) method

Syntax: public synchronized void setMenuBar(MenuBar mb)

Description: The setMenuBar(MenuBar) method of the Frame class sets the generic
                 menu bar for a particular frame to a specified menu bar. The mb parameter
                 indicates the menu bar you want to set.

```
myFrame.setLayout(new BorderLayout());

MenuBar menuBar = new MenuBar();
myFrame.setMenuBar(menuBar);
```

setResizable(boolean) method

Syntax: public void setResizable(boolean resizable)

Description: The setResizable(boolean) method of the Frame class sets the resizable
                 flag. Because this method is Boolean, it returns True when the flag is
                 resizable and False when the flag is not resizable.

```
myFrame.setResizable(true); // make the frame resizable
// or
myFrame.setResizable(false); // make the frame fixed size
```

setTitle(String) method

Syntax: public void setTitle(String title)

Description: The setTitle(String) method of the Frame class sets the generic title of a
                 frame to a specified title. The title parameter indicates the new title you
                 want the frame to have.

```
Frame myFrame = new Frame();
myFrame.setTitle("This is My Title");
```

Frame

Graphics Class

Description: The Graphics class enables you to draw lines, shapes, images, and characters on-screen, which can be used in applets.

Constructors

Graphics() constructor

Syntax: protected Graphics()

Description: The Graphics() constructor of the Graphics class creates (or constructs) a new Graphics object. You cannot directly create graphics contexts. You must obtain them from other graphics contexts or create them from another component.

Methods

clearRect(int, int, int, int) method

Syntax: public abstract void clearRect(int x, int y, int width, int height)

Description: The clearRect(int, int, int, int) method of the Graphics class instructs Java to clear (fill with the current background color of the current drawing surface) a specified rectangle. The drawing surface Java uses depends on the graphics context. The x parameter indicates the x coordinate of the rectangle you want to clear. The y parameter indicates the y coordinate of the rectangle you want to clear. The width parameter indicates the width of the rectangle you want to clear. The height parameter indicates the height of the rectangle you want to clear.

```
public void paint(Graphics g) {
    g.fillOval(100, 100, 100, 100);
    g.clearRect(150, 150, 50, 50);
}
```

clipRect(int, int, int, int) method

Syntax: public abstract void clipRect(int x, int y, int width, int height)

Description: The clipRect(int, int, int, int) method of the Graphics class clips (sets graphics display boundaries) to a rectangle. The intersection of the current clipping area and the rectangle you specify is the affected clipping area. Any graphics operations you perform that are outside of the clipping area have no effect. The x parameter indicates the x coordinate of the rectangle you want to clip, and the y parameter indicates the y coordinate of the rectangle you want to clip. The width parameter indicates the width of the rectangle you want to clip, and the height parameter indicates the height of the rectangle you want to clip.

```
public void paint(Graphics g) {
    g.clipRect(150, 100, 25, 100);
    g.fillOval(100, 100, 100, 100);
    g.clearRect(150, 150, 50, 50);
}
```

copyArea(int, int, int, int, int, int) method

Syntax: public abstract void copyArea(int x, int y, int width, int height, int dx, int dy)

Description: The copyArea(int, int, int, int, int, int) method of the Graphics class copies a specified on-screen area. The x parameter indicates the x coordinate of the area you want to copy, and the y parameter indicates the y coordinate of the area you want to copy. The width parameter indicates the width of the area you want to copy, and the height parameter indicates the height of the area you want to copy. The dx parameter indicates the horizontal distance of the area you want to copy, and the dy parameter indicates the vertical distance of the area you want to copy.

```
public void paint(Graphics g) {
    g.fillOval(100, 100, 100, 100);
    g.clearRect(150, 150, 50, 50);
    g.copyArea(150, 100, 25, 50, 75, 0);
}
```

create() method

Syntax: public abstract Graphics create()

Description: The create() method of the Graphics class creates a copy of an original Graphics object.

create(int, int, int, int) method

Syntax: public Graphics create(int x, int y, int width, int height)

Description: The create(int, int, int, int) method of the Graphics class creates a copy of an original Graphics object. The create(int, int, int, int) method translates the parameters you specify to the appropriate source coordinates, and then clips the Graphics object you just created to a specified area. The x parameter indicates the x coordinate of the Graphics object you want to create. The y parameter indicates the y coordinate of the Graphics object you want to create. The width parameter indicates the width of the Graphics object you want to create. The height parameter indicates the height of the Graphics object you want to create.

```
public void paint(Graphics g) {
    Graphics newG = g.create(150, 100, 25, 100);
    newG.fillOval(0, 0, 100, 100);
    newG.clearRect(50, 50, 50, 50);
    newG.dispose();
    g.copyArea(150, 100, 25, 50, -75, 0);
}
```

dispose() method

Syntax: public abstract void dispose()

Description: The dispose() method of the Graphics class deletes specified graphics context. The graphics context cannot be used once it is deleted.

```
public void paint(Graphics g) {
    Graphics newG = g.create(150, 100, 25, 100);
    newG.fillOval(0, 0, 100, 100);
    newG.clearRect(50, 50, 50, 50);
    newG.dispose();
    g.copyArea(150, 100, 25, 50, -75, 0);
}
```

draw3DRect(int, int, int, int, boolean) method

Syntax: public void draw3DRect(int x, int y, int width, int height, boolean raised)

Description: The draw3DRect(int, int, int, int, boolean) method of the Graphics class
                 enables you to draw a highlighted 3D rectangle. The x parameter indicates
                 the x coordinate of the 3D rectangle you want to draw. The y parameter
                 indicates the y coordinate of the 3D rectangle you want to draw. The width
                 parameter indicates the width of the rectangle you want to draw. The height
                 parameter indicates the height of the rectangle you want to draw. The
                 raised parameter indicates whether the rectangle is raised.

```
public void paint(Graphics g) {
    g.draw3DRect(0, 0, 100, 100, true);
}
```

drawArc(int, int, int, int, int, int) method

Syntax: public abstract void drawArc(int x, int y, int width, int height, int
                 startAngle, int arcAngle)

Description: The drawArc(int, int, int, int, int, int) method of the Graphics class
                 enables you to draw an arc that is bounded by a specified rectangle, from
                 startAngle to endAngle. The 3 o'clock position is 0 degrees. Use

counter-clockwise rotations to draw positive arc angles. Use clockwise rotations to draw negative arc angles. The x parameter indicates the x coordinate of the arc. The y parameter indicates the y coordinate of the arc. The height parameter indicates the height of the rectangle. The startAngle parameter indicates the beginning angle. The arcAngle parameter indicates the angle of the arc you want to draw. This parameter is relative to the startAngle parameter.

```
public void paint(Graphics g) {
    g.drawArc(50, 50, 100, 100, 225, 90);
}
```

drawBytes(byte[], int, int, int, int) method

Syntax: public void drawBytes(byte data[], int offset, int length, int x, int y)

Description: The drawBytes(byte[], int, int, int, int) method of the Graphics class enables you to draw specified bytes, using the current color and font. The data parameter indicates the data you want to draw. The offset parameter indicates the start offset in the data. The length parameter indicates the number of bytes you want to draw. The x parameter indicates the x coordinate of the bytes you want to draw. The y parameter indicates the y coordinate of the bytes you want to draw.

```
public void paint(Graphics g) {
    byte [] byteArray = new byte[3];
    byteArray[0] = 'A';
    byteArray[1] = 'b';
    byteArray[2] = 'C';
    g.drawBytes(byteArray, 0, 3, 25, 25);
}
```

drawChars(char[], int, int, int, int) method

Syntax: public void drawChars(char data[], int offset, int length, int x, int y)

Description: The drawChars(char[], int, int, int, int) method of the Graphics class enables you to draw using the current color and font of the characters you specify. The data parameter indicates the array of characters you want to draw. The offset parameter indicates in the data the start offset. The length parameter indicates the number of characters you want to draw. The x parameter indicates the x coordinate of the place you want to begin. The y parameter indicates the y coordinate of the place you want to begin.

```
public void paint(Graphics g) {
    char [] charArray = new char[3];
    charArray[0] = 'd';
    charArray[1] = 'E';
    charArray[2] = 'f';
    g.drawChars(charArray, 0, 3, 25, 50);
}
```

drawImage(Image, int, int, Color, ImageObserver) method

Syntax: public abstract boolean drawImage(Image img, int x, int y, Color bgcolor, ImageObserver observer)

Description: The drawImage(Image, int, int, Color, ImageObserver) method of the Graphics class enables you to draw an image, starting from the top left corner, that contains the solid background color of your choice. Using this method does not enable you to resize the image you draw. The img parameter indicates the image you want to draw. The x parameter indicates the x coordinate from which you want to begin the image. The y parameter indicates the y coordinate from which you want to begin the image. The observer parameter indicates whether the image is complete.

```
public void paint(Graphics g) {
     Color red = Color.getColor("red", 0xffff0000);
     g.drawImage(myImage, 100, 150, red, this);
}
```

drawImage(Image, int, int, ImageObserver) method

Syntax: public abstract boolean drawImage(Image img, int x, int y, ImageObserver observer)

Description: The drawImage(Image, int, int, ImageObserver) method of the Graphics class enables you to draw an image, starting from the top left corner. Using this method does not enable you to resize the image you draw. The img parameter indicates the image you want to draw. The x parameter indicates the x coordinate from which you want to begin the image. The y parameter indicates the y coordinate from which you want to begin the image. The observer parameter indicates whether the image is complete.

```
public void paint(Graphics g) {
     g.drawImage(myImage, 100, 150, this);
}
```

drawImage(Image, int, int, int, int, Color, ImageObserver) method

Syntax: public abstract boolean drawImage(Image img, int x, int y, int width, int height, Color bgcolor, ImageObserver observer)

Description: The drawImage(Image, int, int, int, int, Color, ImageObserver) method of the Graphics class enables you to draw an image with a solid background color of your choice. This method also enables you to expand or compress the image to fit the space you specify. If the image is larger than the width and height you specify for the bounding box, Java automatically scales the image to fit; however, there may be some degradation of the image due to the scaling. The img parameter indicates the image you want to draw. The x parameter indicates the x coordinate of the image. The y parameter indicates the y coordinate of the image. The width parameter indicates the width of the bounding box. The height coordinate indicates the height of the bounding box. The bgcolor parameter indicates the color you want as the background for your image. The observer parameter indicates whether the image is complete.

```
public void paint(Graphics g) {
       Color red = Color.getColor("red", 0xffff0000);
       g.drawImage(myImage, 100, 150, 20, 30, red, this);
}
```

drawImage(Image, int, int, int, int, ImageObserver) method

Syntax: public abstract boolean drawImage(Image img, int x, int y, int width, int height, ImageObserver observer)

Description: The drawImage(Image, int, int, int, int, ImageObserver) method of the Graphics class enables you to draw an image that can be expanded or compressed to fit within a specified space. If the image is larger than the width and height you specify for the bounding box, Java automatically scales the image to fit; however, there may be some degradation of the image due to the scaling. The img parameter indicates the image you want to draw. The x parameter indicates the x coordinate of the image. The y parameter indicates the y coordinate of the image. The width parameter indicates the width of the bounding box. The height coordinate indicates the height of the bounding box. The observer parameter indicates whether the image is complete.

```
public void paint(Graphics g) {
    g.drawImage(myImage, 100, 150, 20, 30, this);
}
```

drawLine(int, int, int, int) method

Syntax: public abstract void drawLine(int x1, int y1, int x2, int y2)

Description: The drawLine(int, int, int, int) method of the Graphics class enables you to draw a straight line between two specified coordinates. This method uses four arguments that indicate the starting and ending coordinates of the line. The x1 parameter indicates the x coordinate where you want the line to begin. The y1 parameter indicates the y coordinate where you want the line to begin. The x2 parameter indicates the x coordinate to which you want the line to extend. The y2 parameter indicates the y coordinate to which you want the line to extend.

```
public void paint(Graphics g) {
    g.drawLine(0, 0, 100, 100);
}
```

drawOval(int, int, int, int) method

Syntax: public abstract void drawOval(int x, int y, int width, int height)

Description: The drawOval(int, int, int, int) method of the Graphics class enables you to draw ovals and ellipses. The x parameter indicates the x coordinate of the top corner of the oval you want to draw. The y parameter indicates the y coordinate of the top corner of the oval you want to draw. The width parameter indicates the width of the oval you want to draw. The height parameter indicates the height of the oval you want to draw.

```
public void paint(Graphics g) {
    g.drawOval(0, 0, 100, 100);
}
```

drawPolygon(int[], int[], int) method

Syntax: public abstract void drawPolygon(int xPoints[], int yPoints[], int nPoints)

Description: The drawPolygon(int[], int[], int) method of the Graphics class enables you
to draw shapes with an unlimited number of sides. You use an array of x
points and y points, starting with one point and drawing a line to the
second point, drawing a line from the second point to the third point, and
so on. The xPoints parameter indicates an array of x points. The yPoints
parameter indicates an array of y points. The nPoints parameter indicates
the total number of points.

```
public void paint(Graphics g) {
    int [] xCoord = new int[6];
    int [] yCoord = new int[6];
    xCoord[0] = 0; yCoord[0] = 0;
    xCoord[1] = 0; yCoord[1] = 100;
    xCoord[2] = 100; yCoord[2] = 100;
    xCoord[3] = 100; yCoord[3] = 50;
    xCoord[4] = 50; yCoord[4] = 50;
    xCoord[5] = 50; yCoord[5] = 0;
    g.drawPolygon(xCoord, yCoord, 6);
}
```

drawPolygon(Polygon) method

Syntax: public void drawPolygon(Polygon p)

Description: The drawPolygon(Polygon) method of the Graphics class enables you to draw a polygon that is defined by a specified point. The p parameter indicates the polygon you specify.

```
public void paint(Graphics g) {
    Polygon p = new Polygon();
    p.addPoint(0, 0);
    p.addPoint(0, 100);
    p.addPoint(100, 100);
    p.addPoint(100, 50);
    p.addPoint(50, 50);
    p.addPoint(50, 0);
    g.drawPolygon(p);
}
```

drawRect(int, int, int, int) method

Syntax: public void drawRect(int x, int y, int width, int height)

Description: The drawRect(int, int, int, int) method of the Graphics class enables you to draw an outline of a specified rectangle in the current color implemented. To draw an outline inside a specified rectangle, use the drawRect(x, y, width-1, height-1) method. The x parameter indicates the x coordinate of the rectangle you want to draw. The y parameter indicates the y coordinate of the rectangle you want to draw. The width parameter indicates the width of the rectangle you want to draw. The height parameter indicates the height of the rectangle you want to draw.

```
public void paint(Graphics g) {
    g.drawRect(0, 0, 100, 100);
}
```

drawRoundRect(int, int, int, int, int, int) method

Syntax: public abstract void drawRoundRect(int x, int y, int width, int height, int arcWidth, int arcHeight)

Description: The drawRoundRect(int, int, int, int, int, int) method of the Graphics class enables you to draw a rectangle with rounded corners in the current color implemented. The x parameter indicates the x coordinate of the rounded rectangle you want to draw. The y parameter indicates the y coordinate of the rounded rectangle you want to draw. The width parameter indicates the width of the rounded rectangle you want to draw. The height parameter indicates the height of the rounded rectangle you want to draw. The arcWidth parameter indicates the horizontal diameter of the arc (all four corners) of the rounded rectangle you want to draw. The arcWidth parameter indicates the vertical diameter of the arc (all four corners) of the rounded rectangle you want to draw.

```
public void paint(Graphics g) {
    g.drawRoundRect(0, 0, 100, 100, 10, 10); // almost square
corners
    g.drawRoundRect(110, 110, 100, 100, 50, 50); // curvier
corners
}
```

drawString(String, int, int) method

Syntax: public abstract void drawString(String str, int x, int y)

Description: The drawString(String, int, int) method of the Graphics class enables you to draw a specified string, implementing the current color and font. The str parameter indicates the string you want to draw. The x parameter indicates the x coordinate of the starting point of the baseline of the string. The y parameter indicates the y coordinate of the starting point of the baseline of the string.

```
public void paint(Graphics g) {
    Font myFont = new Font("Helvetica", Font.ITALIC, 24);
    String myString = "Draw This String";

    g.setFont(myFont);
    g.drawString(myString, 5, height + 5);
}
```

fill3DRect(int, int, int, int, boolean) method

Syntax: public void fill3DRect(int x, int y, int width, int height, boolean raised)

Description: The fill3DRect(int, int, int, int, boolean) method of the Graphics class paints a highlighted 3D rectangle in the current color used. The x parameter indicates the x coordinate of the rectangle you want to paint. The y parameter indicates the y coordinate of the rectangle you want to paint. The width parameter indicates the width of the rectangle you want to paint. The height parameter indicates the height of the rectangle you want to paint. The raised parameter indicates whether the rectangle is raised.

```
public void paint(Graphics g) {
    g.fill3DRect(0, 0, 100, 100, true);
}
```

fillArc(int, int, int, int, int, int) method

Syntax: public abstract void fillArc(int x, int y, int width, int height, int startAngle, int arcAngle)

Description: The fillArc(int, int, int, int, int, int) method of the Graphics class fills an arc with the current color used. Using this method creates a pie-shaped arc. The x parameter indicates the x coordinate of the arc. The y parameter indicates the y coordinate of the arc. The width parameter indicates the width of the arc. The height parameter indicates the height of the arc. The startAngle parameter indicates the beginning angle. The arcAngle parameter indicates the angle of the arc you are filling. This parameter is relative to the startAngle parameter.

```
public void paint(Graphics g) {
    g.fillArc(50, 50, 100, 100, 225, 90);
}
```

fillOval(int, int, int, int) method

Syntax: public abstract void fillOval(int x, int y, int width, int height)

Description: The fillOval(int, int, int, int) method of the Graphics class fills an oval within a specified rectangle with the current color in use. The x parameter indicates the x coordinate of the oval you want to fill. The y parameter indicates the y coordinate of the oval you want to fill. The width parameter indicates the width of the rectangle. The height parameter indicates the height of the rectangle.

```
public void paint(Graphics g) {
    g.fillOval(0, 0, 100, 100);
}
```

fillPolygon(int[], int[], int) method

Syntax: public abstract void fillPolygon(int xPoints[], int yPoints[], int nPoints)

Description: The fillPolygon(int[], int[], int) method of the Graphics class instructs Java to fill a specified polygon using the even-odd fill (or alternating) rule. The xPoints parameter indicates an array of *x* points. The yPoints parameter indicates an array of *y* points. The nPoint parameter indicates the total number of points.

```
public void paint(Graphics g) {
    int [] xCoord = new int[6];
    int [] yCoord = new int[6];
    xCoord[0] = 0; yCoord[0] = 0;
    xCoord[1] = 0; yCoord[1] = 100;
    xCoord[2] = 100; yCoord[2] = 100;
    xCoord[3] = 100; yCoord[3] = 50;
    xCoord[4] = 50; yCoord[4] = 50;
    xCoord[5] = 50; yCoord[5] = 0;
    g.fillPolygon(xCoord, yCoord, 6);
}
```

fillPolygon(Polygon) method

Syntax: public void fillPolygon(Polygon p)

Description: The fillPolygon(Polygon) method of the Graphics class fills a specified polygon with the current color in use. The p parameter indicates the polygon you want to fill.

```
public void paint(Graphics g) {
    Polygon p = new Polygon();
    p.addPoint(0, 0);
    p.addPoint(0, 100);
    p.addPoint(100, 100);
    p.addPoint(100, 50);
    p.addPoint(50, 50);
    p.addPoint(50, 0);
    g.fillPolygon(p);
}
```

fillRect(int, int, int, int) method

Syntax: public abstract void fillRect(int x, int y, int width, int height)

Description: The fillRect(int, int, int, int) method of the Graphics class fills a specified
rectangle with the current color in use. The x parameter indicates the x
coordinate of the rectangle. The y parameter indicates the y coordinate of
the rectangle. The width parameter indicates the width of the rectangle you
want to fill, and the height parameter indicates the height of the rectangle
you want to fill.

```
public void paint(Graphics g) {
    g.fillRect(0, 0, 100, 100);
}
```

fillRound Rect(int, int, int, int, int, int) method

Syntax: public abstract void fillRound Rect(int x, int y, int width, int height, int
arcWidth, int arcHeight)

Description: The fillRound Rect(int, int, int, int, int, int) method of the Graphics class
enables you to draw a rectangle with rounded corners and fill in the

rectangle with the current color in use. The x parameter indicates the x coordinate of the rectangle. The y parameter indicates the y coordinate of the rectangle. The width parameter indicates the width of the rectangle. The height parameter indicates the height of the rectangle. The arcWidth parameter indicates the horizontal diameter of the arc and the four corners. The arcHeight parameter indicates the horizontal parameter of the arc at the four corners.

```
public void paint(Graphics g) {
    g.fillRoundRect(110, 110, 100, 100, 50, 50);
}
```

finalize() method

Syntax: public void finalize()

Description: The finalize() method of the Graphics class gets rid of a specified graphics context when it is not referenced any more. This method is called automatically by the garbage collector.

getClipRect() method

Syntax: public abstract Rectangle get ClipRect()

Description: The getClipRect() method of the Graphics class returns the bounding rectangle of the current clipping area.

```
Rectangle r = g.getClipRect();
```

getColor() method

Syntax: public abstract Color getColor()

Description: The getColor() method of the Graphics class returns the current color of the graphics you specify.

```
Color currentColor = g.getColor();
System.out.println("The current color is " +
    currentColor.toString());
```

getFont() method

Syntax: public abstract Font getFont()

Description: The getFont() method of the Graphics class returns the current font of the graphics context.

```
Font currentFont = g.getFont();
System.out.println("The current font is " +
    currentFont.toString());
```

getFontMetrics() method

Syntax: public FontMetrics getFontMetrics()

Description: The getFontMetrics() method of the Graphics class returns the present font metrics of the current font.

```
Font myFont = new Font("Helvetica", Font.ITALIC, 24);
g.setFont(myFont);
// now get the metrics for the current font (myFont)
FontMetrics myMetrics = g.getFontMetrics();
```

getFontMetrics(Font) method

Syntax: public abstract FontMetrics getFontMetrics(Font f)

Description: The getFontMetrics(Font) method of the Graphics class returns the current font metrics for a specified font. The f parameter indicates the font you specify.

```
Font myFont = new Font("Helvetica", Font.ITALIC, 24);
FontMetrics myMetrics = g.getFontMetrics(myFont);
```

setFont(Font) method

Syntax: public abstract void setFont(Font font)

Description: The setFont(Font) method of the Graphics class predetermines the font for all following text-drawing operations you perform. The font parameter indicates the font you want to use.

```
Font myFont = new Font("Helvetica", Font.ITALIC, 24);
g.setFont(myFont);
```

setPaintMode() method

Syntax: public abstract void setPaintMode()

Description: The setPaintMode() method of the Graphics class establishes the default paint mode so that it overwrites the destination you specify with the current color in use.

```
public void paint(Graphics g) {
    g.setPaintMode();
    // ...
}
```

setXORMode(Color) method

Syntax: public abstract void setXORMode(Color cl)

Description: The setXORMode(Color) method of the Graphics class sets the paint mode so that it alternates between the current color and the new color you specify. When you perform drawing operations after invoking this method, pixels that are the current color change to the color you specify in the setXORMode(Color) method. The cl parameter indicates the new color you want to use.

```
public void paint(Graphics g) {
    Color red = Color.getColor("red", 0xffff0000);
    g.setXORMode(red);
    // ...
}
```

toString() method

Syntax: public String toString()

Description: The toString() method of the Graphics class returns the String object that represents the value of the graphics you specify. Using this method overrides the toString method in the Object class.

```
System.out.println("The graphics context is " +
    g.toString());
```

translate(int, int) method

Syntax: public abstract void translate(int x, int y)

Description: The translate(int, int) method of the Graphics class instructs Java to translate the parameters you specify into the origin of the graphics context. Any following operations you perform on this graphics context are relative to this particular origin. The x parameter indicates the x coordinate of the specified graphics. The y parameter indicates the y coordinate of the specified graphics.

```
public void paint(Graphics g) {
    g.translate(100, 100);
    // ...
}
```

GridBagConstraints Class

Description: The GridBagConstraints class is used in conjunction with the GridBagLayout class to specify complex arrangements of GUI components in a window. This class is used to specify the orientation, spacing, and size of a component in relation to other components in a window managed by the GridBagLayout layout manager.

Constructors

GridBagConstraints() constructor

Syntax: public GridBagConstraints()

Description: The GridBagConstraints() constructor of the GridBagConstraints class positions a component within a container.

```
GridBagConstraints gbc = new GridBagContstraints();
```

Methods

clone() method

Syntax: public Object clone()

Description: The clone() method of the GridBagConstraints class creates a clone of a specified object.

```
GridBagConstraints newGbc = gbc.clone();
```

Variables

anchor variable

Syntax: public int anchor

Description: The anchor variable of the GridBagConstraints class specifies the way in
                 which you want to display a component within its grid cells when the
                 component is smaller than the cells. The default value for this variable is
                 CENTER.

BOTH variable

Syntax: public final static int BOTH

Description: The BOTH variable of the GridBagConstraints class specifies that a
                 component that is smaller than its display area fills the entire display area.

CENTER variable

Syntax: public final static int CENTER

Description: The CENTER variable of the GridBagConstraints class specifies the way
                 in which you want to display a component within its grid cells when the
                 component is smaller than the cells. CENTER is the default value.

EAST variable

Syntax: public final static int EAST

Description: The EAST variable of the GridBagConstraints class specifies the way in which you want to display a component within its grid cells when the component is smaller than the cells. The default value is CENTER.

fill variable

Syntax: public int fill

Description: The fill variable of the GridBagConstraints class specifies the components you want to expand when the component is smaller than its grid cells.

gridheight variable

Syntax: public int gridheight

Description: The gridheight variable of the GridBagConstraints class specifies the number of cells in a column (the height) of a component within a container. The gridheight default value is 1. To specify that a component be the last one in a particular column, use GridBagConstraintsREMAINDER. To specify that a component be placed next to the adjacent component in the column, use GridBagConstraintsRELATIVE.

gridwidth variable

Syntax: public int gridwidth

Description: The gridwidth variable of the GridBagConstraints class specifies the number of cells in a row (the width) of a component within a container. The gridwidth default value is 1. To specify that a component be the last one in a particular row, use GridBagConstraintsREMAINDER. To specify that a component be placed next to the adjacent component in the row, use GridBagConstraintsRELATIVE.

gridx variable

Syntax: public int gridx

Description: The gridx variable of the GridBagConstraints class specifies the grid position within a container for the component you want to place in the upper left corner of the display area. To specify that Java place the component just to the right of (gridx) or just below (gridy) the component that was added immediately before the action you are performing, use GridBagConstraintsRELATIVE.

gridy variable

Syntax: public int gridy

Description: The gridy variable of the GridBagConstraints class specifies the grid position within a container for the component you want to place in the upper left corner of the display area. To specify that Java place the component just to the right of (gridx) or just below (gridy) the component that was added immediately before the action you are performing, use GridBagConstraintsRELATIVE.

HORIZONTAL variable

Syntax: public final static int HORIZONTAL

Description: The HORIZONTAL variable of the GridBagConstraints class specifies that the component be wide enough horizontally to fill the display area within grid cells when the component is smaller than the cells.

insets variable

Syntax: public Insets insets

Description: The insets variable of the GridBagConstraints class specifies the margins that should appear around the component.

ipadx variable

Syntax: public int ipadx

Description: The ipadx variable of the GridBagConstraints class specifies the internal pad (in pixels) you want to add to the x sides (right and left) of the component. This variable adds padding to both sides of the component and increases the size of the x sides of the component beyond the minimum default size.

ipady variable

Syntax: public int ipady

Description: The ipady variable of the GridBagConstraints class specifies the internal
pad (in pixels) you want to add to the y sides (top and bottom) of the
component. This variable adds padding to both sides of the component and
increases the size of the y sides of the component beyond the minimum
default size.

NONE variable

Syntax: public final static int NONE

Description: The NONE variable of the GridBagConstraints class enables you to specify
that you do not want to enlarge the component to fit within a display area
of grid cells when the component is smaller than the cells. This variable is
the default.

NORTH variable

Syntax: public final static int NORTH

Description: The NORTH variable of the GridBagConstraints class specifies the way in
which you want to display a component within its grid cells when the
component is smaller than the cells. The default value is CENTER.

NORTHEAST variable

Syntax: public final static int NORTHEAST

Description: The NORTHEAST variable of the GridBagConstraints class specifies the way in which you want to display a component within its grid cells when the component is smaller than the cells. The default value is CENTER.

NORTHWEST variable

Syntax: public final static int NORTHWEST

Description: The NORTHWEST variable of the GridBagConstraints class specifies the way in which you want to display a component within its grid cells when the component is smaller than the cells. The default value is CENTER.

RELATIVE variable

Syntax: public final static int RELATIVE

Description: The RELATIVE variable of the GridBagConstraints class specifies that a component be located adjacent to the component that you placed immediately before placing this component.

REMAINDER variable

Syntax: public final static int REMAINDER

Description: The REMAINDER variable of the GridBagConstraints class instructs Java to place a particular component in the last row or column you specify.

SOUTH variable

Syntax: public final static int SOUTH

Description: The SOUTH variable of the GridBagConstraints class specifies the way in which you want to display a component within its grid cells when the component is smaller than the cells. The default value is CENTER.

SOUTHEAST variable

Syntax: public final static int SOUTHEAST

Description: The SOUTHEAST variable of the GridBagConstraints class specifies the way in which you want to display a component within its grid cells when the component is smaller than the cells. The default value is CENTER.

GridBagConstraints

SOUTHWEST variable

Syntax: public final static int SOUTHWEST

Description: The SOUTHWEST variable of the GridBagConstraints class specifies the
way in which you want to display a component within its grid cells when
the component is smaller than the cells. The default value is CENTER.

VERTICAL variable

Syntax: public final static int VERTICAL

Description: The VERTICAL variable of the GridBagConstraints class specifies that the
component be tall enough vertically to fill the display area within grid cells
when the component is smaller than the cells.

weightx variable

Syntax: public double weightx

Description: The weightx variable of the GridBagConstraints class specifies the amount
of space you want to distribute to the components in a row within a container. Because the default weight is zero, you must specify a weight for at
least one component in a row to avoid clustering components within a
container.

weighty variable

Syntax: public double weighty

Description: The weighty variable of the GridBagConstraints class specifies the amount of space you want to distribute to the components in a column within a container. Because the default weight is zero, you must specify a weight for at least one component in a column to avoid clustering components within a container.

WEST variable

Syntax: public final static int WEST

Description: The WEST variable of the GridBagConstraints class specifies the way in which you want to display a component within its grid cells when the component is smaller than the cells. The default value is CENTER.

GridBagLayout Class

Description: The GridBagLayout layout manager is by far the most complex, but is also the most powerful of Java's layout managers. While the FlowLayout class simply places one item after another in a row and the GridLayout class constrains you to a very rigid arrangement of same-sized cells, the GridBagLayout class enables you to have more control over the arrangement of awt components, including the relative size, spacing, and orientation amongst components.

Constructors

GridBagLayout() constructor

Syntax: public GridBagLayout()

Description: The GridBagLayout() constructor of the GridBagLayout class creates a gridbag layout, vertically and horizontally arranging and aligning components of different sizes. This layout manager uses a rectangular grid of cells for the display area. Each component placed takes up one or more cells. The GridBagLayout manager uses specified instances of the GridBagConstraints class to stipulate the way in which a component will be arranged in a display area.

```
GridBagLayout gridBag = new GridBagLayout();
```

Methods

addLayoutComponent(String, Component) method

Syntax: public void addLayoutComponent(String name, Component comp)

Description: The addLayoutComponent(String, Component) method of the
GridBagLayout class adds a specified component to another component
within a layout. The name parameter indicates the name of the component
to which you are adding another component. The comp parameter indicates
the component you want to add. This method is called automatically when
the components are layed out. It would not be called directly by an applet
or application.

AdjustForGravity(GridBagConstraints, Rectangle) method

Syntax: protected void AdjustForGravity(GridBagConstraints constraints,
Rectangle r)

Description: The AdjustForGravity(GridBagConstraints, Rectangle) method of the
GridBagLayout class adjusts the x and y coordinates of the rectangle, based
on the GridBagConstraint's anchor and fill variables. This method should
not be called as it is protected.

ArrangeGrid(Container) method

Syntax: protected void ArrangeGrid(Container parent)

Description: The ArrangeGrid(Container) method of the GridBagLayout class specifies that a new grid be set up exactly as the parent container is set up. The parent parameter indicates the parent you want to duplicate.

defaultConstraints method

Syntax: protected GridBagConstraints defaultConstraints

Description: The defaultConstraints method of the GridBagLayout class returns the default constraints for a particular grid (display area).

DumpConstraints(GridBagConstraints) method

Syntax: protected void DumpConstraints(GridBagConstraint constraints)

Description: The DumpConstraints(GridBagConstraints) method of the GridBagLayout class prints the current constraints for a specified layout. This method is particularly useful when debugging. The constraints parameter indicates the constraints you want to print.

DumpLayoutInfo(GridBagLayoutInfo) method

Syntax: protected void DumpLayoutInfo(GridBagLayoutInfo s)

Description: The DumpLayoutInfo(GridBagLayoutInfo) method of the GridBagLayout class prints the layout information you specify. This method is valuable when debugging. The s parameter indicates the size information you want to print.

getConstraints(Component) method

Syntax: public GridBagConstraints getConstraints(Component comp)

Description: The getConstraints(Component) method of the GridBagLayout class returns the current constraints for a specified component. The comp parameter indicates the component for which you want the constraints.

```
GridBagConstraints gbc =
↪gridBag.getConstraints(myButton);
```

getLayoutDimensions() method

Syntax: public int[][] getLayoutDimensions()

Description: The getLayoutDimensions() method of the GridBagLayout class returns the layout dimensions for a specified grid (display area).

```
int[][] dims = gridBag.getLayoutDimensions();
```

GridBagLayout

GetLayoutInfo(Container, int) method

Syntax: protected GridBagLayoutInfo GetLayoutInfo(Container parent, int
              sizeflag)

Description: The GetLayoutInfo(Container, int) method of the GridBagLayout class
              returns information about the display area of a specified container.

getLayoutOrigin() method

Syntax: public Point getLayoutOrigin()

Description: The getLayoutOrigin() method of the GridBagLayout class returns the
              original layout for a grid.

```
Point p = gridBag.getLayoutOrigin();
```

getLayoutWeights() method

Syntax: public double[][] getLayoutWeights()

Description: The getLayoutWeights() method of the GridBagLayout class returns the
              original weights (spacing of a display area) of a specified layout.

```
double[][] weights = gridBag.getLayoutWeights();
```

GetMinSize(Container, GridBagLayoutInfo) method

Syntax: protected Dimension GetMinSize(Container parent, GridBagLayoutInfo info)

Description: The GetMinSize(Container, GridBagLayoutInfo) method of the GridBagLayout class returns the minimum size of a specified parent and the minimum size of a specified display area. The parent parameter indicates the original container. The info parameter indicates the layout that you are querying.

layoutContainer(Container) method

Syntax: public void layoutContainer(Container parent)

Description: The layoutContainer(Container) method of the GridBagLayout class lays out a container in a specified panel. The parent parameter indicates the component you want to lay out. This method is called automatically when the components are laid out; it should not be called directly by an applet or application.

location(int, int) method

Syntax: public Point location(int x, int y)

Description: The location(int, int) method of the GridBagLayout class specifies the location in a component grid. The x parameter indicates the x coordinate (row) of the cell. The y parameter indicates the y coordinate (column) of the cell.

```
Point p = gridBag.location(2, 3);
```

lookupConstraints(Component) method

Syntax: protected GridBagConstraints lookupConstraints(Component comp)

Description: The lookupConstraints(Component) method of the GridBagLayout class returns the constraints for a specified component. The values that are returned are the actual constraints class the layout mechanism uses. The comp parameter indicates the component for which you want to get the constraints.

minimumLayoutSize(Container) method

Syntax: public Dimension minimumLayoutSize(Container parent)

Description: The minimumLayoutSize(Container) method of the GridBagLayout class returns the minimum dimensions required to lay out components that are within a specified panel. The parent parameter indicates the component you want to lay out. This method is called automatically when the components are laid out; it should not be called directly by an applet or application.

preferredLayoutSize(Container) method

Syntax: public Dimension preferredLayoutSize(Container parent)

Description: The preferredLayoutSize(Container) method of the GridBagLayout class returns the best dimensions for a particular layout. This returned size is based on the existing components within that area. The parent parameter indicates the component you want to lay out. This method is called automatically when the components are laid out; it should not be called directly by an applet or application.

removeLayoutComponent(Component) method

Syntax: public void removeLayoutComponent(Component comp)

Description: The removeLayoutComponent(Component) method of the GridBagLayout class removes a specified component from a particular layout. The comp parameter indicates the component you want to remove. This method is called automatically when the components are layed out; it should not be called directly by an applet or application.

setConstraints(Component, GridBagConstraints) method

Syntax: public void setConstraints(Component comp, GridBagConstraints constraints)

Description: The setConstraints(Component, GridBagConstraints) method of the GridBagLayout class sets constraints for a specified component. The Comp parameter indicates the component for which you want to set the constraints. The constraints parameter indicates the constraints you want to apply to the component.

GridBagLayout

```
GridBagLayout gridBag = new GridBagLayout();
this.setLayout(gridBag);
GridBagContstraints gbc = new GridBagConstraints();
gbc.gridx = 0;
gbc.gridy = 0;
gbc.gridwidth = 1;
gbc.gridheight = 1;
gbc.weightx = 100;
gbc.weighty = 100;
gridBag.setContraints(myLabel, gbc);
this.add(myLabel);
```

toString() method

Syntax: public String toString()

Description: The toString() method of the GridBagLayout class returns the String
representation of the values of the grid layout you specify.

```
System.out.println("The layout is " +
        gridBag.toString());
```

Variables

comptable variable

Syntax: protected Hashtable comptable

Description: The comptable variable of the GridBagLayout class specifies the hashtable
values you want to retrieve.

MAXGRIDSIZE variable

Syntax: protected final static int MAXGRIDSIZE

Description: The MAXGRIDSIZE variable of the GridBagLayout specifies that the display area (grid) be the maximum size allowed.

MINSIZE variable

Syntax: protected final static int MINSIZE

Description: The MINSIZE variable of the GridBagLayout class determines the minimum size you want a layout to be.

PREFERREDSIZE variable

Syntax: protected final static int PREFERREDSIZE

Description: The PREFERREDSIZE variable of the GridBagLayout class determines the best size for a display area. This returned size is based on the existing components within that area.

GridBagLayout

GridLayout Class

Description: The GridLayout class provides a layout manager that enables you to lay out grids within a container.

Constructors

GridLayout(int, int) constructor

Syntax: public GridLayout(int rows, int cols)

Description: The GridLayout(int, int) constructor of the GridLayout class creates a grid layout that contains rows and columns you specify. The rows parameter indicates the rows you want in the grid layout. The cols parameter indicates the columns you want in the grid layout.

```
GridLayout grid = new GridLayout(2, 3);
```

GridLayout(int, int, int, int) constructor

Syntax: public GridLayout(int rows, int cols, int hgap, int vgap)

Description: The GridLayout(int, int, int, int) constructor of the GridLayout class creates a grid layout that contains rows, columns, horizontal gaps, and vertical gaps you specify. The rows parameter indicates the rows you want to add, for which 0 means any number. The cols parameter indicates the columns you want to add, for which 0 means any number. You can only use 0 for either the rows parameter or the columns parameter; you cannot use 0 for both parameters at the same time. The hgap parameter indicates the amount of horizontal gap you want between the columns. The vgap parameter indicates the amount of vertical gap you want between rows. Using this method throws the IllegalArgumentException error when the values for the rows and columns parameters are invalid.

```
GridLayout grid = new GridLayout(2, 3, 5, 5);
```

Methods

addLayoutComponent(String, Component) method

Syntax: public void addLayoutComponent(String name, Component comp)

Description: The addLayoutComponent(String, Component) method of the GridLayout class adds a particular component to another component within a specified layout. The name parameter indicates the name of the component to which you want to add another component. The comp parameter indicates the component you want to add to the string of the first component. This method is called automatically when the components are laid out; it should not be called directly by an applet or application.

layoutContainer(Container) method

Syntax: public void layoutContainer(Container parent)

Description: The layoutContainer(Container) method of the GridLayout class lays out a container in a specified panel. The parent parameter is the component you want to lay out. This method is called automatically when the components are laid out; it should not be called directly by an applet or application.

GridLayout

minimumLayoutSize(Container) method

Syntax: public Dimension minimumLayoutSize(Container parent)

Description: The minimumLayoutSize(Container) method of the GridLayout class returns the minimum dimensions you need to lay out components that are within a specified panel. The parent parameter indicates the component you want to lay out. This method is called automatically when the components are laid out; it should not be called directly by an applet or application.

preferredLayoutSize(Container) method

Syntax: public Dimension preferredLayoutSize(Container parent)

Description: The preferredLayoutSize(Container) method of the GridLayout class returns the most desirable dimensions for a particular layout, considering the components within the specified panel. The parent parameter indicates the component you want to lay out. This method is called automatically when the components are laid out; it should not be called directly by an applet or application.

removeLayoutComponent(Component) method

Syntax: public void removeLayoutComponent(Component comp)

Description: The removeLayoutComponent(Component) method of the GridLayout class removes a specified component from a particular layout. The comp parameter indicates the component you want to remove. This method is called automatically when the components are laid out; it should not be called directly by an applet or application.

toString() method

Syntax: public String toString()

Description: The toString() method of the GridLayout class returns the String representation of the values of the grid layout you specify.

```
System.out.println("The layout is " +
        grid.toString());
```

Image Class

Description: The Image class manages bitmap images. This class provides tools that enable you to crop images, manage and translate pixel color values, modify RGB (red, blue, green) values of pixels in RGB images, and so on.

Methods

flush() method

Syntax: public abstract void flush()

Description: The flush() method of the Image class clears a portion of memory that an Image object is using. The information to be cleared can include system resources being used to store pixels or data for an image, and cached pixel data that will be used to render the image to the screen. Using this method resets the image to a state similar to the original state. If you want to render the modified image, you will need to recreate it or reobtain it from the original source.

getGraphics() method

Syntax: public abstract Graphics getGraphics()

Description: The getGraphics() method of the Image class instructs a graphics object to draw into a particular image. You can only use this method for off-screen images.

getHeight(ImageObserver) method

Syntax: public abstract int getHeight(ImageObserver observer)

Description: The getHeight(ImageObserver) method of the Image class returns the
                  height of an image. In instances when the height information is not known,
                  the ImageObserver is notified at a later time and Java returns –1. The
                  observer parameter indicates whether the image is complete.

getProperty(String, ImageObserver) property method

Syntax: public abstract Object getProperty(String name, ImageObserver observer)

Description: The getProperty(String, ImageObserver) method of the Image class returns,
                  by name, a property of an specified image. Image formats define individual
                  property names. When a property for a particular image is not defined, this
                  method returns the UndefinedProperty object. When properties for the
                  image you want are yet unknown, the getProperty(String, ImageObserver)
                  method returns null and the ImageObserver object is notified later. You
                  should use the "comment" property name to store additional comments for
                  the user, such as a description of the image, the creator of an image, and so
                  on. The name parameter indicates the String representation of the property
                  you want to access. The observer parameter indicates whether the image is
                  complete.

getSource() method

Syntax: public abstract ImageProducer getSource()

Description: The getSource() method of the Image class returns an object that produces
                 pixels for the image you specify. This information is used by the Image
                 filtering class and by the code that handles image conversion and scaling.

getWidth(ImageObserver) method

Syntax: public abstract int getWidth(ImageObserver observer)

Description: The getWidth(ImageObserver) method of the Image class returns the width
                 of an image you specify. When the width is yet unknown, Java notifies the
                 ImageObserver at a later time and returns −1. The observer parameter
                 indicates whether the image is complete.

Variables

UndefinedProperty variable

Syntax: public final static Object UndefinedProperty

Description: Java returns the UndefinedProperty variable of the Image class when it
                 returns an undefined property for a particular image.

Insets Class

Description: The Insets class enables you to lay out containers and sections of containers within containers.

Constructors

Insets(int, int, int, int) constructor

Syntax: public Insets(int top, int left, int bottom, int right)

Description: The Insets(int, int, int, int) constructor of the Insets class constructs and initializes a new Inset that contains top, bottom, left, and right insets you specify. The top parameter indicates the specified top inset. The left parameter indicates the specified left inset. The bottom parameter indicates the specified bottom inset. The right parameter indicates the specified right inset.

Methods

clone() method

Syntax: public Object clone()

Description: The clone() method of the Insets class creates a clone of an object.

Insets

toString() method

Syntax: public String toString()

Description: The toString() method of the Insets class returns a String object that represents the values of a specified Inset. This method overrides the toString() method in the Object class.

Variables

bottom variable

Syntax: public int bottom

Description: The bottom variable of the Insets class specifies the inset from the bottom of the container.

left variable

Syntax: public int left

Description: The left variable of the Insets class specifies the inset from the left of the container.

right variable

Syntax: public int right

Description: The right variable of the Insets class specifies the inset from the right of the container.

top variable

Syntax: public int top

Description: The top variable of the Insets class specifies the inset from the top of the container.

Insets

Label Class

Description: The Label class enables you to create a text label for a specified component. The label alignment and content is designated by the implemented
method or variable.

Constructors

Label() constructor

Syntax: public Label()

Description: The Label() constructor of the Label class creates a label that contains no
text.

Label(String) constructor

Syntax: public Label(String label)

Description: The Label(String) constructor of the Label class creates a new label and
specifies the string of text you want the label to contain. The label parameter indicates the text you want the label to include.

Label(String, int) constructor

Syntax: public Label(String label, int alignment)

Description: The Label(String, int) constructor of the Label class creates a new label that has a String of text and alignment you specify. The label parameter indicates the String to make up the label. The alignment parameter indicates the alignment value the label, such as center, right, left, and so on.

Methods

addNotify() method

Syntax: public synchronized void addNotify()

Description: The addNotify() method of the Label class creates a peer for a specified label. Using a peer enables you to modify the appearance of the label without changing its original functionality.

getAlignment() method

Syntax: public int getAlignment()

Description: The getAlignment() method of the Label class returns the alignment value used for a particular label, such as center, right, or left.

Label

getText() method

Syntax: public String getText()

Description: The getText() method of the Label class returns the text used for a particular label.

paramString() method

Syntax: protected String paramString()

Description: The paramString() method of the Label class returns the parameter String of a particular label. Using this method overrides the paramString method in the Component class.

setAlignment(int) method

Syntax: public void setAlignment(int alignment)

Description: The setAlignment(int) method of the Label class specifies the alignment to be used for a particular label. The alignment parameter indicates the alignment values for the label, such as left, center, or right. If you enter an incorrect value for the alignment parameter, Java throws the IllegalArgumentException error.

setText(String) method

Syntax: public void setText(String label)

Description: The setText(String) method of the Label class sets the text for a particular label. The label parameter indicates the text you want to use for the label.

Variables

CENTER variable

Syntax: public final static int CENTER

Description: The CENTER variable of the Label class indicates that you want to center-align a label.

LEFT variable

Syntax: public final static int LEFT

Description: The LEFT variable of the Label class indicates that you want to left-align a label.

RIGHT variable

Syntax: public final static int RIGHT

Description: The RIGHT variable of the Label class indicates that you want to right-align a label.

Label

List Class

Description: The List class creates scrolling lists (a list of strings), which are lists of items from which a user can choose one or more items. When the list is too long to display in a list box in its entirety, a scrollbar will appear, enabling the user to view all the list items. You can create a scrolling list that will accept the selection of one item at a time or multiple items simultaneously.

Constructors

List() constructor

Syntax: public List()

Description: The List() constructor of the List class creates a new scrolling list that contains no visible lines and limits the user to selecting only one item at a time.

```
List databases = new List();
```

List(int, boolean) constructor

Syntax: public List(int rows, boolean multipleSelections)

Description: The List(int, boolean) constructor of the List class creates a new scrolling list that contains a specified number of visible lines (rows). This method also specifies whether the user can select more than one item at a time. The rows parameter indicates the number of rows (visible lines) you want in the list. The multipleSelections parameter indicates whether the user will be able to select more than one row at a time. True indicates that you want the user to be able to make multiple selections and False indicates that you do not want to provide this capability.

```
List databases = new List(4, false);
```

Methods

addItem(String) method

Syntax: public synchronized void addItem(String item)

Description: The addItem(String) method of the List class adds a specified item to the end of a scrolling list. The item parameter indicates the string of the item you want to add.

```
List databases = new List(4, false);
databases.addItem("Personnel");
databases.addItem("Purchasing");
databases.addItem("Information Systems");
databases.addItem("News");
```

addItem(String, int) method

Syntax: public synchronized void addItem(String item, int index)

Description: The addItem(String, int) method of the List class adds a specified item to the end of an existing list. The item parameter indicates the item you want to add to the end of the scrolling list. The index parameter indicates the position or location in the list in which you want to place the new item. This index (position) is zero-based. When the index is –1, the item will be added to the end of the list. When the index is greater than the number of items in the list, Java adds the item to the end of the list.

```
List databases = new List(4, false);
// list databases in alphabetical order
databases.addItem("Personnel", 0); // first position
databases.addItem("Purchasing", -1); // last position
databases.addItem("Information Systems", 0); // before all the
➡others
databases.addItem("News", 1); // second position
```

addNotify() method

Syntax: public synchronized void addNotify()

Description: The addNotify() method of the List class creates a peer for a particular list. A peer enables you to alter the on-screen appearance of a list while keeping the functionality of the list intact. This method overrides the addNotify method in the Component class.

allowsMultipleSelections() method

Syntax: public boolean allowsMultipleSelections()

Description: The allowsMultipleSelections() method of the List class indicates whether you want a user to be allowed to select more than one item at a time from a list. Because this method is Boolean, you use True to indicate that you want to provide the user the capability to select more than one item at a time from the list and False to indicate that you do not want to provide this capability.

```
if (myList.allowsMultipleSelections()) {
     System.out.println("myList allows multiple selections.");
} else {
     System.out.println("myList does not allow multiple
     ➡selections.");
}
```

clear() method

Syntax: public synchronized void clear()

Description: The clear() method of the List class specifies that a list be cleared of selected items.

```
myMenu.clear();
myMenu.addItem("Books");
myMenu.addItem("Periodicals");
```

List

countItems() method

Syntax: public int countItems()

Description: The countItems() method of the List determines the number of items in a list.

```
System.out.println("myList contains " +
      Integer.toString(myList.countItems()) +
    "items");
```

delItem(int) method

Syntax: public synchronized void delItem(int position)

Description: The delItem(int) method of the List class deletes an item from a list. The position parameter indicates the place in which the item on the list is located.

```
myList.delItem(0); // delete the first item in the list
```

delItems(int, int) method

Syntax: public synchronized void delItems(int start, int end)

Description: The delItems(int, int) method of the List class deletes more than one item
at a time from a list. The start parameter indicates the place from which
you want to begin the deletion process. The end parameter indicates the last
item in the list you want to delete. All items between the start and end
items are included in the deletion process.

```
myList.delItems(1, 3); // delete the second through
➥fourth items
```

deselect(int) method

Syntax: public synchronized void deselect(int index)

Description: The deselect(int) method of the List class instructs Java to deselect a
particular item at a specified index (position of the item). The index
parameter indicates the position of the item you want to deselect.

```
myList.deselect(2); // deselect the third item in the
➥list
```

getItem(int) method

Syntax: public String getItem(int index)

Description: The getItem(int) method of the List class returns an item that correlates with a specified index (the single value interpreted as an absolute value). The index parameter indicates the position of the item you want to get.

```
System.out.println("The third item in the list is " +
        myList.getItem(2));
```

getRows() method

Syntax: public int getRows()

Description: The getRows() method of the List class returns the number of lines in a list that appear on-screen at the same time.

```
System.out.println("The list can display " +
        Integer.toString(myList.getRows()) +
        " rows at a time.");
```

getSelectedIndex() method

Syntax: public synchronized int getSelectedIndex()

Description: The getSelectedIndex() method of the List class returns a selected index
from a list. When no item on a list is selected, Java returns −1.

```
int index = myList.getSelectedIndex();
if (index >= 0) {
    System.out.println("You selected the item " +
        myList.getItem(index));
}
```

getSelectedIndexes() method

Syntax: public synchronized int[] getSelectedIndexes()

Description: The getSelectedIndexes() method of the List class returns selected indexes
from a list.

```
int [] indexes = myList.getSelectedIndexes();
int index;
for (index = 0; index < indexes.length; index++) {
    System.out.println("You selected the item " +
        myList.getItem(index));
}
```

List

getSelectedItem() method

Syntax: public synchronized String getSelectedItem()

Description: The getSelectedItem() method of the List class returns a selected item from a list. If you do not select an item, Java returns null.

```
System.out.println("You selected the item " +
    myList.getSelectedItem());
```

getSelectedItems() method

Syntax: public synchronized String[] getSelectedItems()

Description: The getSelectedItems() method of the List class returns selected items from a list.

```
System.out.println("You selected the items:");
String [] strings = myList.getSelectedItems();
int index;
for (index = 0; index < strings.length; index++) {
    System.out.println(strings[index]);
}
```

getVisibleIndex() method

Syntax:　　　public int getVisibleIndex()

Description:　The getVisibleIndex() method of the List class returns the index of the item you last made visible using the makeVisible method.

```
myList.makeVisible(3);
int visibleIndex = myList.getVisibleIndex(); // will be 3
```

isSelected(int) method

Syntax:　　　public synchronized boolean isSelected(int index)

Description:　The isSelected(int) method of the List class determines whether an item at a specified index (position) is selected. Because this method is Boolean, it returns True when the item is selected and False when the item is not selected. The index parameter indicates the position of the item you are querying.

```
if (myList.isSelected(3)) {
    System.out.println("Deselecting item 3");
    myList.deselect(3);
}
```

makeVisible(int) method

Syntax: public void makeVisible(int index)

Description: The makeVisible(int) method of the List class specifies that a particular index appear on-screen. The index parameter indicates the position of the item that you want to make visible on-screen.

```
myList.makeVisible(3);
int visibleIndex = myList.getVisibleIndex(); // will be 3
```

minimumSize() method

Syntax: public Dimension minimumSize()

Description: The minimumSize() method of the List returns the minimum dimensions you need for the list you want to create. This method returns the best size, and contains the specified number of rows when the row size is greater than zero.

```
Dimension d = myList.minimumSize();
```

minimumSize(int) method

Syntax: public Dimension minimumSize(int rows)

Description: The minimumSize(int) method of the List class returns the minimum
dimensions required for the number of rows in a list. The rows parameter
indicates the minimum number of rows in the list.

```
Dimension d = myList.minimumSize(4);
```

paramString() method

Syntax: protected String paramString()

Description: The paramString() method of the List class returns the parameter string of a
specified list. This method overrides the paramString method in the Component class.

```
System.out.println("myList's parameter string is " +
    myList.paramString());
```

preferredSize() method

Syntax: public Dimension preferredSize()

Description: The preferredSize() method of the List class determines the best dimensions required for a particular list. When the row size is greater than 0, this method returns the most desirable size and includes the specific number of rows.

```
Dimension d = myList.preferredSize();
```

preferredSize(int) method

Syntax: public Dimension preferredSize(int rows)

Description: The preferredSize(int) method of the List class determines the best dimensions required for a list that contains a specific number of rows. The rows parameter indicates the number of rows in the list.

```
Dimension d = myList.preferredSize();
```

removeNotify() method

Syntax: public synchronized void removeNotify()

Description: The removeNotify() method of the List class removes a peer for a particu-
                   lar list. A peer enables you to alter the appearance of the list while retaining
                   the functionality of the list. This method overrides the removeNotify
                   method of the Component class.

replaceItem(String, int) method

Syntax: public synchronized void replaceItem(String newValue, int index)

Description: The replaceItem(String, int) method of the List class replaces a particular
                   item at a specified index (location) with a new value of your discretion. The
                   newValue parameter indicates the new value with which you want to
                   replace the existing item. The index parameter indicates the position of the
                   item you want to replace.

```
List myList = new List();
myList.addItem("Information Systems");
myList.addItem("News");
myList.addItem("Personnel");
myList.addItem("Purchasing");
// ...
// replace "Personnel" with "Human Resources"
myList.replaceItem("Human Resources", 2);
```

List

select(int) method

Syntax: public synchronized void select(int index)

Description: The select(int) method of the List class selects an item that is located at a specified index. The index parameter indicates the position of the item you want to select.

```
List myList = new List();
myList.addItem("Information Systems");
myList.addItem("News");
myList.addItem("Personnel");
myList.addItem("Purchasing");
myList.select(2); // select "Personnel"
```

setMultipleSelections(boolean) method

Syntax: public void setMultipleSelections(boolean v)

Description: The setMultipleSelections(boolean) method of the List class specifies whether you want a user to be able to select more than one item at a time from a list. The v parameter indicates True for allowing multiple selections and False for not allowing multiple selections.

```
List myList = new List();
myList.setMultipleSelections(true); // allow multiple selections
```

MediaTracker Class

Description: Java's MediaTracker class enables you to track and load the status of media objects, such as images. The MediaTracker class makes it possible for you to assign ID numbers to facilitate identifying and tracking media objects. This class enables you to load several images at the same time while specifying that the images be successfully and completely loaded before being used. This class also provides methods and variables that you can use to determine whether images have loaded successfully, whether they experienced errors while loading, or whether the loading process was aborted. Using this class, you also can add images, check the ID of the image, and so on.

Constructors

MediaTracker(Component) constructor

Syntax: public MediaTracker(Component comp)

Description: The MediaTracker(Component) constructor of the MediaTracker class creates a media tracker for images of a specified component. The comp parameter indicates the component on which you eventually want to draw the images you are tracking.

```
myTracker = new MediaTracker(this);
```

Methods

addImage(Image, int) method

Syntax: public void addImage(Image image, int id)

Description: The addImage(Image, int) method of the MediaTracker class adds an image to a list of images you are tracking. Java renders the image you add to its unscaled, default size. The image parameter indicates the image you want to track. The id parameter indicates the ID of the image you want to use to track the image at a later date.

```
myTracker = new MediaTracker(this);
int index;
for (index = 0; index < imageArray.length; index++) {
    myTracker.addImage(imageArray[index], index);
}
```

addImage(Image, int, int, int) method

Syntax: public synchronized void addImage(Image image, int id, int w, int h)

Description: The addImage(Image, int, int, int) method of the MediaTracker class adds a scaled image to a list of images you are tracking. Java will render the image to your size specifications. The image parameter indicates the image you want to add to be tracked. The id parameter indicates the identification you want to assign to the image for tracking in the future. The w parameter indicates the width you want the image to be. The h parameter indicates the height you want the image to be.

```
myTracker = new MediaTracker(this);
int index;
for (index = 0; index < imageArray.length; index++) {
    myTracker.addImage(imageArray[index], index, 100, 100);
}
```

checkAll() method

Syntax: public boolean checkAll()

Description: The checkAll() method of the MediaTracker class determines whether all
the images have completed the loading process; however, this method does
not enable you to specify that the loading process begin. In this circumstance, "complete" does not imply the successful loading of an image in
that it is ready for use. The image is considered complete when the image
is successfully loaded or when an error while loading or scaling occurs. To
check for errors, use isErrorAny() or isErrorID(). This method returns True
when the loading process is complete, aborted, or encounters an error.

```
if (myTracker.checkAll()) {
    System.out.println("Loading completed");
}
```

checkAll(boolean) method

Syntax: public synchronized boolean checkAll(boolean load)

Description: The checkAll(boolean) method of the MediaTracker class determines
whether images queued in the loading procedure have completed the
process. Because this method is Boolean (the load parameter), it returns

True when the loading process is complete, aborted, or experiences an error, and False when the loading process is incomplete. In this circumstance, "complete" does not imply the successful loading of an image in that it is ready for use. The image is considered complete when the image successfully loads or when an error while loading or scaling occurs. To check for loading errors, use isErrorAny or isErrorID.

```
if (myTracker.checkAll(true)) {
    System.out.println("Loading completed");
} else {
    System.out.println("Still loading");
}
```

checkID(int) method

Syntax: public boolean checkID(int id)

Description: The checkID(int) method of the MediaTracker class determines whether the loading of images labeled with the indicated ID is complete, or whether the images have started the loading process. In this circumstance, "complete" does not imply the successful loading of an image in that it is ready for use. The id parameter indicates the identifier you want to use to specify the images you want to check. Because this method is Boolean, it returns True when all tagged images complete the loading process, abort, or when an error occurs.

```
if (myTracker.checkId(1)) {
    if (myTracker.isErrorID(1)) {
        System.err.println("Error loading image 1");
    } else {
        System.out.println("Image 1 loaded successfully");
    }
}
```

checkID(int id, boolean load) method

Syntax: public synchronized boolean checkID(int id, boolean load)

Description: The checkID(int id, boolean load) method of the MediaTracker determines whether the images you tagged with a specific ID have completed the loading process. If the load parameter indicates True, then Java begins to load any remaining images that contain the specified ID. In this circumstance, "complete" does not imply the successful loading of an image in that it is ready for use. The image is considered complete when the image successfully loads or when an error while loading or scaling occurs. To check for errors, use isErrorAny() or isErrorID(). The id parameter indicates the identifier you want to use to determine the images you want to check. The load parameter indicates whether to start loading the images (True to load or False to not load). This method returns True when all images you tagged are loaded, aborted, or when an error occurs.

```
if (myTracker.checkId(1)) {
    if (myTracker.isErrorID(1)) {
        System.err.println("Error loading image 1");
    } else {
        System.out.println("Image 1 loaded successfully");
    }
} else {
    System.out.println("Still loading image 1");
}
```

getErrorsAny() method

Syntax: public synchronized Object[] getErrorsAny()

Description: The getErrorsAny() method of the MediaTracker class returns an array of media objects that have encountered or experienced errors while loading. If no errors were encountered, Java returns null.

```
Object [] errObjects = myTracker.getErrorsAny();
.if (errObjects) {
    int index;
    for (index = 0; index < errObjects.length; index++) {
        System.err.println("Error loading " +
                errObjects[index].toString());
    }
}
```

getErrorsID(int) method

Syntax: public synchronized Object[] getErrorsID(int id)

Description: The getErrorsID(int) method of the MediaTracker class returns a list of
media objects with specified IDs that have encountered errors. The id
parameter indicates the identifier you use to specify which media objects
you query. This method returns an array of objects. If no errors occur, this
method returns null.

```
Object [] errObjects = myTracker.getErrorsID(1);
if (errObjects) {
    int index;
    for (index = 0; index < errObjects.length; index++) {
        System.err.println("Error loading " +
                errObjects[index].toString());
    }
}
```

isErrorAny() method

Syntax: public synchronized boolean isErrorAny()

Description: The isErrorAny() method of the MediaTracker class checks the error status for all images you are loading. Because this method is Boolean, it returns True when any image experiences an error during loading.

```
if (myTracker.isErrorAny()) {
    System.err.println("Errors occcurred loading the images");
}
```

isErrorID(int) method

Syntax: public synchronized boolean isErrorID(int id)

Description: The isErrorID(int) method of the MediaTracker class checks the error status of all the images that contain a specified ID. The id parameter indicates the images you want to check. This method returns True if any of the images you IDed encounter an error during loading.

```
if (my Tracker.isErrorID(1)) {
    System.err.println("Errors occurred loading the series 1
    ➥images");
}
```

statusAll(boolean) method

Syntax: public int statusAll(boolean load)

Description: The statusAll(boolean) method of the MediaTracker class tracks whether
                 media is loading. The load parameter indicates whether you want to start
                 the loading process, such as True to load and False to not begin the loading
                 process.

```
if (myTracker.statusAll(true) & MediaTracker.ERRORED) {
    System.err.println("Errors occurred in loading images");
}
```

statusID(int, boolean) method

Syntax: public int statusID(int id, boolean load)

Description: The statusID(int, boolean) method of the MediaTracker class returns the
                 Boolean OR of the status of all images that contain a specified ID. The id
                 parameter indicates the particular identifier you want to assign to an image
                 in order to track it in the future. The load parameter indicates whether to
                 begin the loading process (True to load or False to not load).

```
if (myTracker.statusID(1, true) & MediaTracker.ERRORED) {
    System.err.println("Error occurred in loading the series 1
    ➥images");
}
```

waitForAll() method

Syntax: public synchronized void waitForAll() throws InterruptedException

Description: The waitForAll() method of the MediaTracker class specifies that images
that are being loaded either complete the loading process or receive an
error before they are rendered. In this circumstance, "complete" does not
imply the successful loading of an image in that it is ready for use. The
image is considered complete when the image successfully loads or when
an error while loading or scaling occurs. To check for loading errors, use
isErrorAny() or isErrorID(). When another thread has interrupted the thread
of the waitForAll() method, Java throws the InterruptedException error.

```
try {
      myTracker.waitForAll();
} catch(InterruptedException e);
```

waitForAll(long) method

Syntax: public synchronized boolean waitForAll(long ms)

Description: The waitForAll(long) method of the MediaTracker class specifies that the
loading process for all images begin and that the loading process is
aborted, throws an error, is completed, or that the process has timed out
before images are rendered. In this circumstance, "complete" does not
imply the successful loading of an image in that it is ready for use. The
image is considered complete when the image successfully loads or when
an error while loading or scaling occurs. To check for loading errors, use
isErrorAny() or isErrorID(). The ms parameter indicates the amount of
time (in milliseconds) to wait for the loading process to complete before
timing out.

```
try {
      if (myTracker.waitForAll(100)) {
            System.out.println("Images successfully loaded");
      }
} catch(InterruptedException e);
```

waitForID(int) method

Syntax: public synchronized void waitForId(int id) throws InterruptedException

Description: The waitForID(int) method of the MediaTracker class specifies that the loading process begins at the image you specify and that Java waits until the loading process is complete before rendering images on-screen. In this circumstance, "complete" does not imply the successful loading of an image in that it is ready for use. The image is considered complete when the image successfully loads or when an error occurs while loading or scaling. To check for loading errors, use isErrorAny() or isErrorID(). The id parameter indicates the identifier you want to use to specify which images to wait for. Java throws the InterruptedException error when the thread of the waitForID(int) method has been interrupted by another thread.

```
try {
      myTracker.waitForID(1);
} catch(InterruptedException e);
```

waitForID(int, long) method

Syntax: public synchronized boolean waitForID(int id, long ms) throws
InterruptedException

Description: The waitForID(int, long) method of the MediaTracker class specifies
images with a particular ID start to load and that Java continues the loading
process until it is complete, an error is received, or the process has timed
out. In this circumstance, "complete" does not imply the successful loading
of an image in that it is ready for use. The image is considered complete
when the image successfully loads or when an error while loading or
scaling occurs. To check for loading errors, use statusID or isErrorID.

```
try {
        if (myTracker.waitForID(1, 100)) {
                System.out.println("Series 1 images loaded success
                ➥fully.");
        }
} catch(InterruptedException e);
```

Variables

ABORTED variable

Syntax: public final static int ABORTED

Description: The ABORTED variable of the MediaTracker class is a flag that indicates
that the download process of an image was aborted.

COMPLETE variable

Syntax: public final static int COMPLETE

Description: The COMPLETE variable of the MediaTracker class is a flag that indicates that the download process of an image was completed successfully.

ERRORED variable

Syntax: public final static int ERRORED

Description: The ERRORED variable of the MediaTracker class is a flag that indicates that the download process of an image encountered an error.

LOADING variable

Syntax: public final static int LOADING

Description: The LOADING variable of the MediaTracker class is a flag that indicates whether media currently is being loaded.

Menu Class

Description: The Menu class enables you to create a pull-down menu that is part of a menu bar.

Constructors

Menu(String) constructor

Syntax: public Menu(String label)

Description: The Menu(String) constructor of the Menu class creates a new menu with a label you specify. This constructor does not allow for a tear-off menu option. A tear-off menu remains on-screen after the user releases the mouse button. The label parameter indicates the label you want on the menu.

```
Menu file = new Menu("File");
```

Menu(String, boolean) constructor

Syntax: public Menu(String label, boolean tearOff)

Description: The Menu(String, boolean) constructor of the Menu class creates a new menu with a label you specify. You also can indicate whether you want the menu to be a tear-off menu by using the Boolean tearOff parameter. The label parameter indicates the label of text you want the menu to contain. The tearOff parameter indicates whether the menu is a tear-off menu—True indicates that it is a tear-off menu and False indicates that it is not.

```
Menu file = new Menu("File", false);
```

Methods

add(MenuItem) method

Syntax: public synchronized MenuItem add(MenuItem mi)

Description: The add(MenuItem) method of the Menu class adds a specified menu item to a particular menu. The mi parameter indicates the menu item you want to add to the menu.

```
Menu file = new Menu("File");
file.add(new MenuItem("New"));
file.add(new MenuItem("Open"));
file.add(new MenuItem("Close"));
file.addSeparator();
file.add(new MenuItem("Exit"));
```

add(String) method

Syntax: public void add(String label)

Description: The add(String) method of the Menu class adds a text string to a menu item on a menu. This is accomplished by specifying the label of the menu item you want to add. The label parameter indicates the text you want to appear on the item.

```
Menu file = new Menu("File");
file.add("New");
file.add("Open");
file.add("Close");
file.addSeparator();
file.add("Exit");
```

addNotify() method

Syntax: public synchronized void addNotify()

Description: The addNotify() method of the Menu class creates a peer of a menu. A peer enables you to alter the appearance of a menu while retaining its functionality. This method overrides the addNotify() method of the MenuItem class.

addSeparator() method

Syntax: public void addSeparator()

Description: The addSeparator() method of the Menu class adds a separator line (hyphen) to the bottom of a menu item at its current position.

```
Menu file = new Menu("File");
file.add("New");
file.add("Open");
file.add("Close");
file.addSeparator();
file.add("Exit");
```

Menu

countItems() method

Syntax: public int countItems()

Description: The countItems() method of the Menu class returns the number of items on
a particular menu.

```
System.out.println("There are " +
      Integer.toString(file.countItems()) +
      " items on the file menu.");
```

getItem(int) method

Syntax: public MenuItem getItem(int index)

Description: The getItem(int) method of the Menu class returns an item that is located at
an index of a specified menu. The index parameter indicates the position of
the menu item queried.

```
System.out.println("The third item on the file menu is " +
      file.getItem(2).toString());
```

isTearOff() method

Syntax: public boolean isTearOff()

Description: The isTearOff() method of the Menu class specifies whether a menu is a tear-off menu. A tear-off menu continues to be visible on-screen after the user releases the mouse button. Because this method is Boolean, a True value specifies that the menu is a tear-off menu and a False value specifies that it is not.

```
if (file.isTearOff()) {
     System.out.println("The file menu is tear-off.");
}
```

remove(int) method

Syntax: public synchronized void remove(int index)

Description: The remove(int) method of the Menu class deletes a menu item from a specified index. The index parameter indicates the position of the menu item you want to delete.

```
file.remove(2); // remove the third item on the menu
```

Menu

remove(MenuComponent) method

Syntax: public synchronized void remove(MenuComponent item)

Description: The remove(MenuComponent) method of the Menu class deletes a specified menu. The item parameter indicates the menu item you want to delete.

```
MenuItem m = file.getItem(2);
file.remove(m); // remove the third item on the menu
```

removeNotify() method

Syntax: public synchronized void removeNotify()

Description: The removeNotify() method of the Menu class eliminates the peer of a
menu. This method overrides the removeNotify method in the
MenuComponent class.

MenuBar Class

Description: The MenuBar class enables you to create a menu bar that is bound to a frame. Menu bars contain menus for the application you are creating. This class compresses the menu bar concept of the platform on which you are working. To conjoin the menu bar with a frame, you need to call the setMenuBar() method from the Frame class.

Constructors

MenuBar() constructor

Syntax: public MenuBar()

Description: The MenuBar() constructor of the MenuBar class creates a new menu bar. Menu bars contain menus for the application you are creating.

```
MenuBar menuBar = new MenuBar();
```

Methods

add(Menu) method

Syntax: public synchronized Menu add(Menu m)

Description: The add(Menu) method of the MenuBar class adds a menu bar to a specified menu. The m parameter indicates the menu you want to add to the menu bar.

```
MenuBar menuBar = new MenuBar();

// the file menu
Menu file = new Menu("File");
file.add(new MenuItem("New"));
file.add(new MenuItem("Open"));
file.add(new MenuItem("Close"));
file.addSeparator();
file.add(new MenuItem("Exit"));

menuBar.add(file);
```

addNotify() method

Syntax: public synchronized void addNotify()

Description: The addNotify() method of the MenuBar creates a peer of a menu bar. A peer enables you to alter the on-screen appearance of a menu bar while retaining its functionality.

countMenus() method

Syntax: public int countMenus()

Description: The countMenus() method of the MenuBar class returns the number of menus a menu bar contains.

```
System.out.println("The menu bar contains " +
    Integer.toString(menuBar.countMenus()) +
    " menus.");
```

getHelpMenu() method

Syntax: public Menu getHelpMenu()

Description: The getHelpMenu() method of the MenuBar class accesses the help menu of a particular menu bar.

```
Menu helpMenu = menuBar.getHelpMenu();
```

getMenu(int) method

Syntax: public Menu getMenu(int i)

Description: The getMenu(int) method of the MenuBar class accesses a specified menu from a selected menubar. The i parameter indicates the menu you want to access.

```
Menu firstMenu = menuBar.getMenu(0);
```

MenuBar

remove(int) method

Syntax: public synchronized void remove(int index)

Description: The remove(int) method of the MenuBar class deletes (removes) a menu located at the specified index from the menu bar. The index parameter indicates the location of the menu bar you want to delete.

```
menuBar.remove(1); // remove the second menu
```

remove(MenuComponent) method

Syntax: public synchronized void remove(MenuComponent m)

Description: The remove(MenuComponent) method of the MenuBar class removes a specified menu from a menu bar. The m parameter indicates the menu you want to remove.

```
MenuComponent firstMenu = menuBar.getMenu(0);
menuBar.remove(firstMenu);
```

removeNotify() method

Syntax: public void removeNotify()

Description: The removeNotify() method of the MenuBar class removes a peer of a menu bar. A peer enables you to alter the on-screen appearance of the menu bar while retaining its functionality. This method overrides the removeNotify method of the MenuComponent class.

setHelpMenu(Menu) method

Syntax: public synchronized void setHelpMenu(Menu m)

Description: The setHelpMenu(Menu) method of the MenuBar class sets a help menu to a menu from the specified menu bar. The m parameter indicates the menu you want to set as the help menu.

MenuComponent Class

Description: The MenuComponent class contains all menu-related classes, such as the Menu class, MenuBar class, and MenuItem class.

Constructors

MenuComponent() constructor

Syntax: public MenuComponent()

Description: The MenuComponent class is an abstract class. Its constructor cannot be called, but is overridden in the subclasses of the MenuComponent class (MenuBar and MenuItem).

Methods

getFont() method

Syntax: public Font getFont()

Description: The getFont() method of the MenuComponent class determines the font used for a particular menu item. When a font is being used, this method returns the font; however, when no font is being used, Java returns null.

MenuComponent

```
MenuComponent mc = this.getMenuBar();
Font mcFont = mc.getFont();
if (mcFont != null) {
    System.out.println("The font for this menu component is " +
        mcFont.toString());
} else {
    System.out.println("The font for this menu component is
    ➥null.");
}
```

getParent() method

Syntax: public MenuContainer getParent()

Description: The getParent() method of the MenuComponent class returns the parent
container.

```
MenuBar myMenuBar = this.getMenuBar();
Menu fileMenu = myMenuBar.getMenu(0);
MenuComponent mc;
for (int itemIndex = 0;
    itemIndex < fileMenu.countItems();
    ++itemIndex) {
    mc = fileMenu.getItem(itemIndex);
    System.out.println("The parent container for this menu item
    ➥is " +
        mc.getParent().toString());
}
```

getPeer() method

Syntax: public MenuComponentPeer getPeer()

Description: The getPeer() method of the MenuComponent class accesses the peer of a
                particular menu component. The peer enables you to alter the appearance
                of the menu component while retaining its functionality.

paramString() method

Syntax: protected String paramString()

Description: The paramString() method of the MenuComponent class returns the String
                parameter of a particular MenuComponent.

```
MenuComponent mc = menu.getItem(0);
System.out.println("The parameter string for this item is " +
    mc.paramString());
```

postEvent(Event) method

Syntax: public void postEvent(Event evt)

Description: The postEvent(Event) method of the MenuComponent class assigns a
                specified event to a menu. The evt parameter indicates the event you want
                to take place.

```
Event myEvt = new Event(this, Event.KEY_RELEASE, this);
file.postEvent(myEvt);
```

MenuComponent

removeNotify() method

Syntax: public void removeNotify()

Description: The removeNotify() method of the MenuComponent class deletes the peer
                of a particular menu component. A peer enables you to alter the on-screen
                appearance of a menu component while retaining its functionality.

setFont(Font) method

Syntax: public void setFont(Font f)

Description: The setFont(Font) method of the MenuBar class specifies the font you want
                to use for a menu item. The f parameter indicates the font you want to use.

```
Font menuFont = new Font("Times-Roman", Font.ITALIC, 24);
MenuBar menuBar = new MenuBar();
menuBar.setFont(menuFont);
```

toString() method

Syntax: public String toString()

Description: The toString() method of the MenuComponent class returns the String
                representation of the values of a particular menu component. This method
                overrides the toString method in the Object class.

```
MenuComponent mc = menu.getItem(0);
System.out.println("This menu item is " + mc.toString());
```

MenuItem Class

Description: The MenuItem class provides individual choices on Java's pull-down menus, such as "Open...", "Close", and "Exit". It is related to the CheckboxMenuItem class, which allows for on/off toggles on menus.

Constructors

MenuItem(String) constructor

Syntax: public MenuItem(String label)

Description: The MenuItem(String) constructor of the MenuItem class creates a new menu item with a text label you specify. The label parameter indicates the text you want to appear on the label.

```
// the file menu
Menu file = new Menu("File");
file.setFont(menuFont);
file.add(new MenuItem("New"));
file.addSeparator();
file.add(new MenuItem("Open"));
file.add(new MenuItem("Close"));
file.addSeparator();
file.add(new MenuItem("Exit"));
```

Methods

addNotify() method

Syntax: public synchronized void addNotify()

Description: The addNotify() method of the MenuItem class creates a peer of a menu
item. A peer enables you to alter the on-screen appearance of a menu item
while retaining its functionality.

disable() method

Syntax: public void disable()

Description: The disable() method of the MenuItem class specifies that a menu item is
not available for the user to select.

```
MenuItem exit = new MenuItem("Exit");
exit.disable(); // "gray out" the exit menu item
file.add(exit);
```

enable() method

Syntax: public void enable()

Description: The enable() method of the MenuItem class specifies that a menu item is
available for user selection.

```
MenuItem print = new MenuItem("print");
print.enable();
file.add(print);
```

enable(boolean) method

Syntax: public void enable(boolean cond)

Description: The enable(boolean) method of the MenuItem class enables a menu item,
                 given certain specified conditions. For example, if the File menu is ac-
                 cessed, then the user can select the Open command (True). The cond
                 parameter indicates the condition that must be met before a particular menu
                 item is enabled.

```
MenuItem exit = new MenuItem("Exit");
exit.enable(false); // "gray out" the exit menu item
file.add(exit);
```

getLabel() method

Syntax: public String getLabel()

Description: The getLabel() method of the MenuItem class returns the text label for a
                 particular menu item.

```
for (int itemIndex = 0; itemIndex < file.countItems();
    ++itemIndex) {
    MenuItem mi = file.getItem(itemIndex);
    if (mi.isEnabled()) {
        System.out.println("Item " + mi.getLabel() + " is
        ➥enabled.");
    } else {
        System.out.println("Item " + mi.getLabel() + " is
        ➥disabled.");
    }
}
```

isEnabled() method

Syntax: public boolean isEnabled()

Description: The isEnabled() method of the MenuItem class specifies whether you want
                 to enable a particular menu item. Because this method is Boolean, a True
                 value enables the menu item and a False value disables the menu item.

```
for (int itemIndex = 0; itemIndex < file.countItems();
    ++itemIndex) {
    MenuItem mi = file.getItem(itemIndex);
    if (mi.isEnabled()) {
        System.out.println("Item " + mi.getLabel() + " is
        ➥enabled.");
    } else {
        System.out.println("Item " + mi.getLabel() + " is
        ➥disabled.");
    }
}
```

paramString() method

Syntax: public String paramString()

Description: The paramString() method of the MenuItem class returns the String
                 parameter of a particular menu item. This method overrides the
                 paramString method in the MenuComponent class.

```
System.out.println("The menu item's parameter string is " +
    myItem.paramString());
```

setLabel(String) method

Syntax: public void setLabel(String label)

Description: The setLabel(String) method of the MenuItem class specifies the text for a
                 particular label.

```
MenuItem print = new MenuItem("Print");
// ...
print.setLabel("Print...");
```

Panel Class

Description: The Panel class is a subclass of the Container class and is used as a container that is contained by another container—in other words, it is a nested container. The Panel class does not create independent windows or frames, but rather contains or holds other components of a parent frame or dialog box. FlowLayout is the default layout manager for this class.

Constructors

Panel() constructor

Syntax: public Panel()

Description: The Panel() constructor of the Panel class creates a new panel to be used as a container. FlowLayout is the default manager for all panels.

```
buttonPanel = new Panel();
buttonPanel.setLayout(new FlowLayout());
buttonPanel.add("OKButton", okButton);
buttonPanel.add(cancelButton);
```

Methods

addNotify() method

Syntax: public synchronized void addNotify()

Description: The addNotify() method of the Panel class creates a peer for a panel. The peer panel enables you to alter the on-screen appearance of a panel while retaining its functionality. This method overrides the addNotify() method of the Container class.

Point Class

Description: The Point class enables you to specify x and y coordinates that meet at a point. This class is useful when creating polygon objects, rectangle objects, and so on. You also can use this class to determine points (x, y) for rectangle and polygon objects.

Constructors

Point(int, int) constructor

Syntax: public Point(int x, int y)

Description: The Point(int, int) consructor of the Point class creates a point, initializing it using specified x and y coordinates. The x parameter indicates the x coordinate of the point you are creating. The y parameter indicates the y coordinate of the point you are creating.

```
Dimension d = new Dimension(10, 10);
Point p = new Point(20, 20);
Rectangle r = Rectangle(p, d);
```

Methods

equals(Object) method

Syntax: public boolean equals(Object obj)

Description: The equals(Object) method of the Point class compares two points and determines whether they are equal. The obj parameter indicates the point of the object you want to compare to the point of another object. Because this method is Boolean, it returns True when the two objects are equal and False when the two objects are unequal.

```
Point p1 = new Point(10, 10);
Point p2 = new Point(10, 10);
Point p3 = new Point(30, 30);
if (p1.equals(p1)) {
    System.err.println("p1 == p1"); // this is true
}
if (p1.equals(p2)) {
    System.err.println("p1 == p2"); // this is true, too
}
if (p1.equals(p3)) {
    System.err.println("p1 == p3"); // this is false
}
```

Point

hashCode() method

Syntax: public int hashCode()

Description: The hashCode() method of the Point class returns the hash code (unique number) for a particular point. You use hash codes to store objects in hash tables. This method overrides the hashcode() method of the Object class. This method is used by the java.util.Hashtable class and would not typically be called in an applet or application.

move(int, int) method

Syntax: public void move(int x, int y)

Description: The move(int, int) method of the Point class moves or repositions a particular point by providing new x and y coordinates. The x parameter indicates
the new x coordinate of the point you are moving. The y parameter indicates the new y coordinate of the point you are moving.

```
Point myPoint = new Point(10, 10);
// ...
myPoint.move(30, 30);
```

toString() method

Syntax: public String toString()

Description: The toString() method of the Point class returns the String representation of
the coordinates of a particular point. This method overrides the toString()
method of the Object class.

```
Point myPoint= new Point(10, 10);
System.out.println("My point is " + myPoint.toString());
```

translate(int, int) method

Syntax: public void translate(int x, int y)

Description: The translate(int, int) method of the Point class adds specified values to
                 particular coordinates, further adjusting the point.

```
Point myPoint = new Point(10, 10);
// ...
myPoint.translate(20, 20); // my points coordinates are now (30,
➥30)
```

Variables

x variable

Syntax: public int x

Description: The x variable of the Point class indicates the x coordinate of the point you
                 are creating or modifying.

y variable

Syntax: public int y

Description: The y variable of the Point class indicates the y coordinate of the point you
                 are creating or modifying.

Point

Polygon Class

Description: The Polygon class enables you to create polygon objects by specifying points or an array of points.

Constructors

Polygon() constructor

Syntax: public Polygon()

Description: The Polygon() constructor of the Polygon class creates a vacant polygon object.

```
Polygon p = new Polygon();
```

Polygon(int[], int[], int) constructor

Syntax: public Polygon(int xpoints[], int ypoints[], int npoints)

Description: The Polygon(int[], int[], int) constructor of the Polygon class creates a polygon object, initializing it using specified parameters. The xpoints parameter indicates the x coordinates of the polygon object you are creating. The ypoints parameter indicates the y coordinates of the polygon object you are creating. The npoints parameter indicates the total number of points used in the polygon object you are creating.

```
int [] xCoord = new int[6];
int [] yCoord = new int[6];
xCoord[0] = 0;    yCoord[0] = 0;
xCoord[1] = 0;    yCoord[1] = 100;
xCoord[2] = 100; yCoord[2] = 100;
xCoord[3] = 100; yCoord[3] = 50;
xCoord[4] = 50;   yCoord[4] = 50;
xCoord[5] = 50;   yCoord[5] = 0;
Polygon p = new Polygon(xCoord, yCoord, 6);
```

Methods

addPoint(int, int) method

Syntax: public void addPoint(int x, int y)

Description: The addPoint(int, int) method of the Polygon class adds or appends a point
to an existing polygon object. When the x and y coordinates are within a
bounding box, this method automatically updates the bounds of the box.
The x parameter indicates the x coordinate of the point you want to add.
The y parameter indicates the y coordinate of the point you want to add.

```
Polygon p = new Polygon();
p.addPoint(0, 0);
p.addPoint(0, 100);
p.addPoint(100, 100);
p.addPoint(100, 50);
p.addPoint(50, 50);
p.addPoint(50, 0);
```

Polygon

getBoundingBox() method

Syntax: public Rectangle getBoundingBox()

Description: The getBoundingBox() method of the Polygon class determines the smallest rectangular area that contains a particular polygon.

```
Polygon p = new Polygon();
p.addPoint(0, 0);
p.addPoint(0, 100);
p.addPoint(100, 100);
p.addPoint(100, 50);
p.addPoint(50, 50);
p.addPoint(50, 0);
Rectangle r = p.getBoundingBox();
```

inside(int, int) method

Syntax: public boolean inside(int x, int y)

Description: The inside(int, int) method of the Polygon class determines whether a point you specify is within a particular polygon object. The x parameter indicates the x coordinate of the point you are testing. The y parameter indicates the y coordinate of the point you are testing.

```
if (myPolygon.inside(10, 10)) {
        System.out.println("The point (10, 10) is inside my
    ↪polygon.");
}
```

Variables

npoints variable

Syntax: public int npoints

Description: The npoints variable of the Polygon class specifies the total number of points in a polygon object.

xpoints variable

Syntax: public int xpoints[]

Description: The xpoints variable of the Polygon class specifies an array of x coordinates for a polygon object.

ypoints variable

Syntax: public int ypoints[]

Description: The ypoints variable of the Polygon class specifies an array of y coordinates for a polygon object.

Polygon

Rectangle Class

Description: The Rectangle class enables you to create and customize rectangle objects according to specified dimensions and initial x and y coordinates. The methods of this class provide information about and functionality to the rectangle objects created.

Constructors

Rectangle() constructor

Syntax: public Rectangle()

Description: The Rectangle constructor of the Rectangle class creates a rectangle object using x and y coordinates, width, and height.

```
Rectangle r = new Rectangle();
```

Rectangle(Dimension) constructor

Syntax: public Rectangle(Dimension d)

Description: The Rectangle(Dimension) constructor of the Rectangle class creates a rectangle, initializing it using specified dimensions. The d parameter indicates the dimensions you want the rectangle to be.

```
Dimension d = new Dimension(20, 30);
Rectangle r = new Rectangle(d); // create a 20 by 30 rectangle
```

Rectangle(int, int) constructor

Syntax: public Rectangle(int width, int height)

Description: The Rectangle(int, int) constructor of the Rectangle class creates a rectangle, initializing it using specified width and height parameters. The width parameter indicates the width you want the rectangle to be. The height parameter indicates the height you want the rectangle to be.

```
Rectangle r = new Rectangle(20, 30); // create a 20 by 30
➥rectangle
```

Rectangle(int, int, int, int) constructor

Syntax: public Rectangle(int x, int y, int width, int height)

Description: The Rectangle(int, int, int, int) constructor of the Rectangle class creates a rectangle, initializing it using specified parameters. The x parameter indicates the x coordinate of the rectangle you are creating. The y parameter indicates the y coordinate of the rectangle you are creating. The width parameter indicates the width you want the rectangle to be. The height parameter indicates the height you want the rectangle to be.

```
// create a new 20 by 30 rectangle at (10, 10)
Rectangle r = new Rectangle(10, 10, 20, 30);
```

Rectangle(Point) constructor

Syntax: public Rectangle(Point p)

Description: The Rectangle(Point) constructor of the Rectangle class creates a rectangle, initializing it at a specified point. The p parameter indicates the point at which you want to initialize the rectangle.

```
Point p = new Point(10, 10);
Rectangle r = new Rectangle(p); // create a new rectangle at
➡(10, 10)
```

Rectangle(Point, Dimension) constructor

Syntax: public Rectangle(Point p, Dimension d)

Description: The Rectangle(Point, Dimension) constructor of the Rectangle class creates a rectangle, initializing it using a specified point and dimensions. The p parameter indicates the point at which you want the rectangle to begin. The d parameter indicates the dimensions you want the rectangle to be.

```
Point p = new Point(10, 10);
Dimension d = new Dimension(20, 30);
// create a new 20 by 30 rectangle at (10, 10)
Rectangle r = new Rectangle(p, d);
```

Methods

add(int, int) method

Syntax: public void add(int x, int y)

Description: The add(int, int) method of the Rectangle class adds a point to a rectangle, resulting in the smallest rectangle that contains both the point and the rectangle. The x parameter indicates the x coordinate of the point you want to add. The y parameter indicates the y coordinate of the point you want to add.

```
Rectangle r = new Rectangle(20, 30);
r.add(10, 10);
```

add(Point) method

Syntax: public void add(Point pt)

Description: The add(Point) method of the Rectangle class adds a point to a rectangle, resulting in the smallest rectangle that contains both the rectangle and the point. The pt parameter indicates the point you want to add.

```
Rectangle r = new Rectangle(20, 30);
Point p = new Point(10, 10);
r.add(p);
```

add(Rectangle) method

Syntax: public void add(Rectangle r)

Description: The add(Rectangle) method of the Rectangle class adds a pre-existing
                rectangle to another rectangle, resulting in the joining of both rectangles.
                The r parameter indicates the pre-existing rectangle you want to add.

```
Rectangle r1 = new Rectangle(10, 10, 20, 30);
Rectangle r2 = new Rectangle(5, 5, 10, 15);
r1.add(r2);
```

equals(Object) method

Syntax: public boolean equals(Object obj)

Description: The equals(Object) method of the Rectangle class compares two rectangles
                to determine whether they are equal. Because this method is Boolean, a
                value of True indicates when the two rectangles you are comparing are
                equal, and a value of False indicates when they are unequal. The obj
                parameter indicates the rectangle you want to compare against.

```
Rectangle r1 = new Rectangle(10, 10, 20, 30);
Point p = new Point(10, 10);
Dimension d = new Dimension(20, 30);
Rectangle r2 = new Rectangle(p, d);
if (r1.equals(r2)) {
    System.out.println("r1 == r2"); // this is true
}
```

grow(int, int) method

Syntax: public void grow(int h, int v)

Description: The grow(int, int) method of the Rectangle class increases the size of the rectangle, expanding the rectangle by h on the left *and* the right and expanding it by v on the top *and* the bottom.

hashCode() method

Syntax: public int hashCode()

Description: The hashCode() method of the Rectangle class assigns a hash code—a unique number—to a rectangle. Hash codes are used when storing objects in a hash table. This method overrides the hashCode() method of the Object class. This method is used by the java.util.Hashtable class and would not typically be called in an applet or application.

inside(int, int) method

Syntax: public boolean inside(int x, int y)

Description: The inside(int, int) method of the Rectangle class determines whether a specified point is contained within a particular rectangle. The x parameter indicates the x coordinate of the point. The y parameter indicates the y coordinate of the point.

```
if (rect.inside(15, 15)) {
    System.out.println("The point (15, 15) is inside the
    ➥rectangle.");
}
```

intersection(Rectangle) method

Syntax: public Rectangle intersection(Rectangle r)

Description: The intersection(Rectangle) method of the Rectangle class returns the
                rectangle that represents the intersection of the two rectangles.

```
Rectangle iRect = r1.intersection(r2);
```

intersects(Rectangle) method

Syntax: public boolean intersects(Rectangle r)

Description: The intersects(Rectangle) method of the Rectangle class determines
                whether two rectangles intersect or overlap. The r parameter indicates the
                rectangle you are comparing against.

```
if (rect1.intersects(rect2)) {
     System.out.println("Rectangle 1 intersects rectangle 2.");
}
```

isEmpty() method

Syntax: public boolean isEmpty()

Description: The isEmpty() method of the Rectangle class determines whether a particu-
                lar rectangle is empty or vacant; that is, whether or not the rectangle has a
                positive width and height. Because this method is Boolean, it returns True
                if the rectangle is empty and False if the rectangle contains objects.

```
Rectangle iRect = r1.intersection(r2);
if (iRect.isEmpty()) {
    System.out.println("r1 and r2 do -not- intersect");
}
```

move(int, int) method

Syntax: public void move(int x, int y)

Description: The move(int, int) method of the Rectangle class moves or repositions a rectangle by specifying new x and y coordinates. The x parameter indicates the new x coordinate of the rectangle you are moving. The y parameter indicates the new y coordinate of the rectangle you are moving.

```
myRect.move(20, 20); // reposition the rectangle
```

reshape(int, int, int, int) method

Syntax: public void reshape(int x, int y, int width, int height)

Description: The reshape(int, int, int, int) method of the Rectangle class modifies the shape of an existing rectangle. You use the x parameter and y parameter to indicate the new x and y coordinates for the rectangle you are modifying. You use the width parameter to indicate the new height you want the rectangle to be. You use the height parameter to indicate the new height you want the rectangle to be.

```
myRect.reshape(20, 20, 40, 50); // change the location
➥and size of the rect
```

resize(int, int) method

Syntax: public void resize(int width, int height)

Description: The resize(int, int) method of the Rectangle class resizes a particular
rectangle, using height and width. The width parameter indicates the new
width you want the rectangle to be. The height parameter indicates the new
height you want the rectangle to be.

```
myRect.resize(40, 50); // resize the rectangle
```

toString() method

Syntax: public String toString()

Description: The toString() method of the Rectangle class returns a String representation
of the values of a particular rectangle. This method overrides the toString()
method of the Object class.

```
System.out.println("The rectangle is " +
➥myRect.toString());
```

translate(int, int) method

Syntax: public void translate(int x, int y)

Description: The translate(int, int) method of the Rectangle class adds specified values to the coordinates of a rectangle. The x parameter indicates the x coordinate of a rectangle. The y parameter indicates the y coordinate of a rectangle.

```
myRect.translate(20, 20);
```

union(Rectangle) method

Syntax: public Rectangle union(Rectangle r)

Description: The union(Rectangle) method of the Rectangle class returns the smallest rectangle containing the two rectangles, which is the geometrical union of the two rectangles.

```
Rectangle uRect = r1.union(r2);
```

Variables

height variable

Syntax: public int height

Description: The height variable of the Rectangle class specifies the height of the rectangle you are creating or modifying.

width variable

Syntax: public int width

Description: The width variable of the Rectangle class specifies the width of a rectangle.

x variable

Syntax: public int x

Description: The x variable of the Rectangle class specifies the x coordinate of a rectangle.

y variable

Syntax: public int y

Description: The y variable of the Rectangle class specifies the y coordinate of a rectangle.

Scrollbar Class

Description: The Scrollbar class enables you to create vertical and horizontal scrollbars with the minimum and maximum values you specify to be used in windows, list boxes, and so on.

Constructors

Scrollbar() constructor

Syntax: public Scrollbar()

Description: The Scrollbar() constructor of the Scrollbar class creates a simple scrollbar in a vertical orientation that has 0, 0 for the initial maximum and minimum values.

```
Scrollbar sBar = new Scrollbar();
```

Scrollbar(int) constructor

Syntax: public Scrollbar(int orientation)

Description: The Scrollbar(int) constructor of the Scrollbar class creates a scrollbar in the orientation (vertical or horizontal) you specify that has 0, 0 for the initial maximum and minimum values.

```
Scrollbar sBar = new Scrollbar(Scrollbar.VERTICAL);
```

Scrollbar(int, int, int, int, int) constructor

Syntax: public Scrollbar(int orientation, int value, int visible, int minimum, int maximum)

Description: The Scrollbar(int, int, int, int, int) method of the Scrollbar class creates a new scrollbar, specifying values such as the orientation of the scrollbar (horizontal or vertical), the value of the scrollbar, the page size, and the number of lines a scrollbar moves up or down (or side to side, depending on the orientation) when receiving user input. The orientation parameter indicates the directional placement of the scrollbar. The value parameter indicates the initial value of the scrollbar, and should be between the minimum and maximum value. The visible parameter indicates the overall width or height (depending on the orientation) of the scrollbar that appears on-screen. The minimum parameter indicates the smallest unit the scrollbar moves up or down (or side to side, depending on the orientation) when receiving user input. The maximum parameter indicates the maximum number of lines a scrollbar will move up or down (or side to side, depending on the orientation) when receiving user input.

```
// create a vertical scrollbar with a visible height of 50
Scrollbar sBar = new Scrollbar(ScrollBar.VERTICAL, 0, 50, 0,
➥500);
```

Methods

addNotify() method

Syntax: public synchronized void addNotify()

Description: The addNotify() method of the Scrollbar class creates a peer of a particular scrollbar. A peer enables you to alter the on-screen appearance of the scrollbar, while retaining its functionality. This method overrides the addNotify() method of the Component class.

getPageIncrement() method

Syntax: public int getPageIncrement()

Description: The getPageIncrement() method of the Scrollbar class determines the page increment in pixels of a particular scrollbar. The page increment is the number of pages that the scrollbar moves up or down when receiving user input.

```
int pageIncrement = sBar.getPageIncrement();
```

getLineIncrement() method

Syntax: public int getLineIncrement(int l)

Description: The getLineIncrement() method of the Scrollbar class determines how many lines a page scrolls up or down in response to user input. The l parameter indicates the number of lines you want the scrollbar to move in response to user input.

```
int lineIncrement = sBar.getLineIncrement();
```

Scrollbar

getMaximum() method

Syntax: public int getMaximum()

Description: The getMaximum() method of the Scrollbar class returns the maximum value for a particular scrollbar. The maximum value refers to the maximum number of lines a scrollbar will move up or down (or side to side, depending on the orientation) when receiving user input.

```
int max = sBar.getMaximum();
```

getMinimum() method

Syntax: public int getMinimum()

Description: The getMinimum() method of the Scrollbar class returns the minimum value of a particular scrollbar.

```
int min = sBar.getMinimum();
```

getOrientation() method

Syntax: public int getOrientation()

Description: The getOrientation() method of the Scrollbar class determines the orientation of a particular scrollbar. The orientation refers to the direction of the scrollbar (vertical or horizontal).

```
int orientation = sBar.getOrientation();
// should be VERTICAL or HORIZONTAL
```

getValue() method

Syntax: public int getValue()

Description: The getValue() method of the Scrollbar class returns the current value of a particular scrollbar. The value is the place in which the scrollbox appears on the scrollbar.

```
int value = sBar.getValue();
```

Scrollbar

getVisible() method

Syntax: public int getVisible()

Description: The getVisible() method of the Scrollbar class returns the value of the
               scrollbar that appears on-screen.

```
int visHeight = sBar.getVisible();
```

paramString() method

Syntax: protected String paramString()

Description: The paramString() method of the Scrollbar class returns the String param-
               eters for a particular scrollbar. This method overrides the paramString()
               method of the Component class.

```
System.out.println("The parameter string for the scrollbar is "
➡+
    sBar.paramString());
```

setLineIncrement(int) method

Syntax: public void setLineIncrement(int l)

Description: The setLineIncrement(int) method of the Scrollbar class specifies the value
               of the line increment (the number of pixels) a particular scrollbar will move

up or down when the user clicks on scroll-up or scroll-down arrows. The l
parameter indicates the number of pixels you want the scrollbar to move up
or down in response to user input.

```
sBar.setLineIncrement(10);
```

setPageIncrement(int) method

Syntax: public void setPageIncrement(int l)

Description: The setPageIncrement(int) method of the Scrollbar class specifies the
number of pixels a particular scrollbar will move up or down when receiving user input. The l parameter indicates the number of pixels you want the
scrollbar to move up or down in response to user input.

```
sBar.setPageIncrement(100);
```

setValue(int) method

Syntax: public void setValue(int value)

Description: The setValue(int) method of the Scrollbar class specifies a value for a
particular scrollbar. The value parameter indicates the position of the
scrollbox on the scrollbar.

```
sBar.setValue(0);
```

Scrollbar

setValues(int, int, int, int) method

Syntax: public void setValues(int value, int visible, int minimum, int maximum)

Description: The setValues(int, int, int, int) method of the Scrollbar class specifies values for a scrollbar, such as the amount of the scrollbar that appears on-screen, number of lines a scrollbar moves when receiving user input, and so on. The value parameter indicates the initial value of the scrollbar, and should be between the minimum and maximum value. The visible parameter indicates how much of the scrollbar appears on-screen. The minimum parameter indicates the smallest unit the scrollbar moves up or down (or side to side, depending on the orientation) when receiving user input. The maximum parameter indicates the maximum number of lines a scrollbar will move up or down (or side to side, depending on the orientation) when receiving user input.

```
sBar.setValues(50, 10, 0, 100); // set the scrollbar in
➥the middle
```

Variables

HORIZONTAL variable

Syntax: public final static int HORIZONTAL

Description: The HORIZONTAL variable of the Scrollbar class specifies that a scrollbar be of a horizontal orientation.

VERTICAL variable

Syntax: public final static int VERTICAL

Description: The VERTICAL variable of the Scrollbar class specifies that a scrollbar be of a vertical orientation.

TextArea Class

Description: The TextArea class enables you to display a TextArea object, which is a multiline area that displays text. You use this class to display text for editing or read-only purposes. You also can specify lines of text, columns, and rows.

Constructors

TextArea() constructor

Syntax: public TextArea()

Description: The TextArea() constructor of the TextArea class creates a new text area.

```
TextArea ta = new TextArea();
```

TextArea(int, int) constructor

Syntax: public TextArea(int rows, int cols)

Description: The TextArea(int, int) constructor of the TextArea class creates a new text area with the number of rows and columns you specify. The rows parameter indicates the number of rows you want the text area to contain. The cols parameter indicates the number of columns you want the text area to contain.

```
TextArea ta = new TextArea(10, 80); // 10 rows of 80
➥columns
```

TextArea(String) constructor

Syntax: public TextArea(String text)

Description: The TextArea(String) constructor of the TextArea class creates a new text
area that contains text you specify. The text parameter indicates the text
you want to appear on-screen.

```
// an initialized text area
TextArea ta = new TextArea("This is my text area.");
```

TextArea(String, int, int) constructor

Syntax: public TextArea(String text, int rows, int cols)

Description: The TextArea(String, int, int) constructor of the TextArea class creates a
new text area that contains the text, rows, and columns you specify. The
text parameter indicates the text you want to appear in the text area. The
rows parameter indicates the number of rows you want the text area to
contain. The cols parameter indicates the number of columns you want the
text area to contain.

```
// an initialized text area with 10 rows of 80 columns
TextArea ta = new TextArea("This is my text area.", 10,
➥80);
```

TextArea

Methods

addNotify() method

Syntax: public synchronized void addNotify()

Description: The addNotify() method of the TextArea class creates a peer of a particular
text area. Creating a peer enables you to alter the on-screen appearance of a
text area while retaining its original functionality. This method overrides
the addNotify method in the Component class.

appendText(String) method

Syntax: public void appendText(String str)

Description: The appendText(String) method of the TextArea class adds text to the end
of another text string. The str parameter indicates the text you want to
insert.

```
textArea.appendText("Add this text to the end of the buffer.");
repaint();
```

getColumns() method

Syntax: public int getColumns()

Description: The getColumns() method of the TextArea class determines the number of
columns in a particular text area.

```
int cols = textArea.getColumns();
System.out.println("The text area contains " +
➥Integer.toString(cols) +
    " columns.");
```

getRows() method

Syntax: public int getRows()

Description: The getRows() method of the TextArea class determines the number of rows in a particular text area.

```
int rows = textArea.getRows();
System.out.println("The text area contains " +
➥Integer.toString(rows) +
    " rows.");
```

insertText(String, int) method

Syntax: public void insertText(String str, int pos)

Description: The insertText(String, int) method of the TextArea class inserts text at a specified position of your choosing. The str parameter indicates the text you want to insert. The pos parameter indicates the location at which you want to insert the text you specify.

```
textArea.insertText("Place this at the front of the
buffer.\n", 0);
```

minimumSize() method

Syntax: public Dimension minimumSize()

Description: The minimumSize() method of the TextArea class returns the minimum size dimensions of a particular text area. This method overrides the minimumSize method of the Component class.

```
Dimension d = textArea.minimumSize();
```

minimumSize(int, int) method

Syntax: public Dimension minimumSize(int rows, int cols)

Description: The minimumSize(int, int) method of the TextArea class determines the minimum size (in pixels) of a text area with a given number of rows and columns.

```
Dimension d = textArea.minimumSize(10, 40);
```

paramString() method

Syntax: protected String paramString()

Description: The paramString() method of the TextArea class returns the string of parameters for a particular text area. This method overrides the paramString() method in the TextComponent class.

```
System.out.println("The parameter string for the text area is "
➡+
        textArea.paramString());
```

preferredSize() method

Syntax: public Dimension preferredSize()

Description: The preferredSize() method of the TextArea class returns the preferred
                 size dimensions of a particular text area. This method overrides the
                 preferredSize() method in the Component class.

```
Dimension d = textArea.preferredSize();
```

preferredSize(int, int) method

Syntax: public Dimension preferredSize(int rows, int cols)

Description: The preferredSize(int, int) method of the TextArea class returns the pre-
                 ferred text area dimensions for the row and column you specify. The rows
                 parameter indicates the preferred number of rows. The cols parameter
                 indicates the preferred number of columns.

```
Dimension d = textArea.preferredSize(10, 40);
```

TextArea

replaceText(String, int, int) method

Syntax: public void replaceText(String str, int start, int end)

Description: The replaceText(String, int, int) method of the TextArea class replaces existing text with new text. You use the str parameter to indicate the new (replacement) text. You use the start parameter to indicate the place in which you want to begin the new text and the end parameter to indicate where you want the new text to end. Using this method overwrites the existing text.

```
// replace the first ten characters of text with "New text"
textArea.replaceText("New text", 0, 9);
```

TextComponent Class

Description: The TextComponent class enables you to edit a text component in a text area. This class does not provide constructors with which you can directly create components; however, this class does provide methods that are common to the two subclasses it contains: the TextArea class and the TextField class.

Methods

getSelectedText() method

Syntax: public String getSelectedText()

Description: The getSelectedText() method of the TextComponent class returns the text you have selected in a particular text component.

```
System.out.println("The selected text is " +
        textArea.getSelectedText());
```

getSelectionEnd() method

Syntax: public int getSelectionEnd()

Description: The getSelectionEnd() method of the TextComponent class returns the end position of text you have selected.

```
int end = textField.getSelectionEnd();
```

TextComponent

getSelectionStart() method

Syntax: public int getSelectionStart()

Description: The getSelectionStart() method of the TextComponent class returns the
start position of text you have selected.

```
int start = textField.getSelectionStart();
```

getText() method

Syntax: public String getText()

Description: The getText() method of the TextComponent class determines the text that
is contained in a particular text component.

```
System.out.println("Your username, " +
    username.getText() + " is invalid.");
```

isEditable() method

Syntax: public boolean isEditable()

Description: The isEditable() method of the TextComponent class determines whether
you are allowed to edit a particular text component. Because this method is

Boolean, it returns True when a text component is editable and False when the text component is not editable.

```
Boolean b = textArea.isEditable();
```

paramString() method

Syntax: protected String paramString()

Description: The paramString() method of the TextComponent class returns the string of parameters for a particular text component. This method overrides the paramString() method in the Component class.

```
System.out.println("The parameter string for the text component
➥is " +
    textArea.paramString());
```

removeNotify() method

Syntax: public synchronized void removeNotify()

Description: The removeNotify() method of the TextComponent class removes the peer of a particular text component. Using a peer enables you to alter the on-screen appearance of a text component while retaining its original functionality. This method overrides the removeNotify() method of the Component class.

select(int, int) method

Syntax: public void select(int selStart, int selEnd)

Description: The select(int, int) method of the TextComponent class selects text that is between a specified start and end position. The setStart parameter indicates the start position of the text you want to select. The selEnd parameter indicates the end position of the text you want to select.

```
textArea.select(0, 9); // select the first 10 characters
➥of the text area
```

selectAll() method

Syntax: public void selectAll()

Description: The selectAll() method of the TextComponent class selects all the text in a particular text component.

```
textField.selectAll(); // select the entire field.
```

setEditable(boolean) method

Syntax: public void setEditable(boolean t)

Description: The setEditable(boolean) method of the TextComponent class sets a Boolean command that indicates whether a user can edit a text component you specify. The t parameter indicates the Boolean you want to set.

```
textArea.setEditable(false); // don't allow user to edit this
➥field
textArea.appendText("The answer is 12.");
```

setText(String) method

Syntax: public void setText(String t)

Description: The setText(String) method of the TextComponent class specifies the existing text you want to appear on-screen. The t parameter indicates the text you want to appear on-screen.

```
textField.setText("type your password here");
```

TextField Class

Description: The TextField class is a subclass of the TextComponent class, which
enables you to create single text fields that contain text, columns, and rows
you specify. This class also enables you to edit a single line of text.

Constructors

TextField() constructor

Syntax: public TextField()

Description: The TextField() constructor of the TextField class creates a new text field.

```
TextField myTextField = new TextField();
```

TextField(int) constructor

Syntax: public TextField(int cols)

Description: The TextField(int) constructor of the TextField class creates a new text
field, initializing it with specified columns. The cols parameter indicates
the number of columns you want the text field to contain.

```
TextField.myTextField = new TextField(10); // 10
➥character text field
```

TextField(String) constructor

Syntax: public TextField(String text)

Description: The TextField(String) constructor of the TextField class creates a new text field that contains text you specify. The text parameter indicates the text you want to appear on-screen.

```
TextField userName = new TextField("type your username here");
userName.selectAll();
```

TextField(String, int) constructor

Syntax: public TextField(String text, int cols)

Description: The TextField(String, int) constructor of the TextField class creates a new text field, initializing it with text and columns you specify. The text parameter indicates the text you want to appear on-screen. The cols parameter indicates the number of columns you want the text field to contain.

```
TextField homePage = new TextField("your URL here", 50);
```

Methods

addNotify() method

Syntax: public synchronized void addNotify()

Description: The addNotify() method of the TextField class creates a peer for a particular text field. Creating a peer enables you to alter the on-screen appearance
of the text field while maintaining its original functionality.

echoCharIsSet() method

Syntax: public boolean echoCharIsSet()

Description: The echoCharIsSet() method of the TextField class determines whether a
character in a text field is set for echoing. Because this method is Boolean,
it returns True when a character is set for echoing and False when a character is not set.

```
if (password.echoCharIsSet()) {
    char echoChar = password.getEchoChar();
    System.out.println("The echo character is " +
            Character(echoChar).toString());
}
```

getColumns() method

Syntax: public int getColumns()

Description: The getColumns() method of the TextField class determines the number of
                columns contained within a particular text field.

```
int numCols = textField.getColumns();
```

getEchoChar() method

Syntax: public char getEchoChar()

Description: The getEchoChar() method of the TextField class returns the character you
                want to use for echoing, such as an asterisk in place of a letter or number in
                the case of a password.

```
System.out.println("The text area contains " +
➥Integer.toString(cols) +
      " columns.");
```

minimumSize() method

Syntax: public Dimension minimumSize()

Description: The minimumSize() method of the TextField class returns the minimum size dimensions required for a particular text field. This method overrides the minimumSize() method of the Component class.

```
Dimension d = textField.minimumSize();
```

minimumSize(int) method

Syntax: public Dimension minimumSize(int cols)

Description: The minimumSize(int) method of the TextField class returns the minimum size dimensions (number of columns) required for a particular text field. The cols parameter indicates the number of columns in this particular text field.

```
Dimension d = textField.minimumSize();
```

paramString() method

Syntax: protected String paramString()

Description: The paramString() method of the TextField class returns the string of parameters for a particular text field. This method overrides the paramString() method f the TextComponent class.

```
System.out.println("The parameter string for the text field is "
➡+
      textField.paramString());
```

preferredSize() method

Syntax: public Dimension preferredSize()

Description: The preferredSize() method of the TextField class determines the preferred size dimensions required for a particular text field. This method overrides the preferredSize() method of the Component class.

```
Dimension d = textField.preferredSize();
```

preferredSize(int) method

Syntax: public Dimension preferredSize(int cols)

Description: The preferredSize(int) method of the TextField class returns the preferred size dimensions (number of columns) required for a particular text field.

The cols parameter indicates the preferred number of columns in this text field.

```
Dimension d = textField.preferredSize(15);
```

setEchoCharacter(char) method

Syntax: public void setEchoCharacter(char c)

Description: The setEchoCharacter(char) method of the TextField class sets the echo character for a particular type of text, such as when creating user password fields in which the text the user types should not appear on-screen. The c parameter indicates the echo character for this particular text field.

```
TextField password = new TextField(15);
password.setEchoCharacter('*'); // echo '*' instead of typed
➥chars
```

Toolkit Class

Description: The Toolkit class enables you to create platform-dependent peers for each java.awt component type. The Toolkit class is provided for each platform to support Java's GUI interface. Do not use the Toolkit methods to create peers for portable programs—use the Component classes for this task. You use the Toolkit class and its subclasses to get screen information, to determine the supported fonts for a particular platform, and to create on-screen elements—such as buttons, images, dialog boxes, and so on—using peers. Creating a peer enables you to alter the on-screen appearance of an object while retaining its original functionality.

Methods

Toolkit

checkImage(Image, int, int, ImageObserver) method

Syntax: public abstract int checkImage(Image image, int width, int height, ImageObserver observer)

Description: The checkImage(Image, int, int, ImageObserver) method of the Toolkit class monitors the status (progress) of a particular image of a specified screen height and width. The image parameter indicates the image you are checking. The width parameter indicates the width of the screen. The height parameter indicates the height of the screen. The observer parameter indicates whether the image is complete.

```
int status = Toolkit.getDefaultToolkit().checkImage(myImage,
    300, 300, this);

if ((status & ImageObserver.ABORT) != 0) {
   System.out.println("Abort");
}
if ((status & ImageObserver.ALLBITS) != 0) {
   System.out.println("AllBits");
}
if ((status & ImageObserver.ERROR) != 0) {
   System.out.println("Error");
}
if ((status & ImageObserver.FRAMEBITS) != 0) {
   System.out.println("FrameBits");
}
if ((status & ImageObserver.HEIGHT) != 0) {
   System.out.println("Height");
}
if ((status & ImageObserver.PROPERTIES) != 0) {
   System.out.println("Properties");
}
if ((status & ImageObserver.SOMEBITS) != 0) {
   System.out.println("SomeBits");
}
if ((status & ImageObserver.WIDTH) != 0) {
   System.out.println("Width");
}
```

createButton(Button) method

Syntax: protected abstract ButtonPeer createButton(Button target)

Description: The createButton(Button) method of the Toolkit class creates a new button
using a specified peer interface. Creating a peer enables you to alter the on-
screen appearance of a button while retaining its original functionality. The
target parameter indicates the new button you want to create.

createCanvas(Canvas) method

Syntax: protected abstract CanvasPeer createCanvas(Canvas target)

Description: The createCanvas(Canvas) method of the Toolkit class creates a new canvas
                 using a specified peer interface. Creating a peer enables you to alter the on-
                 screen appearance of a canvas while retaining its original functionality. The
                 target parameter indicates the new canvas you want to create.

createCheckbox(Checkbox) method

Syntax: protected abstract CheckboxPeer createCheckbox(Checkbox target)

Description: The createCheckbox(Checkbox) method of the Toolkit class creates a new
                 checkbox using a specified peer interface. Creating a peer enables you to
                 alter the on-screen appearance of a checkbox while retaining its original
                 functionality. The target parameter indicates the new checkbox you want to
                 create.

createCheckboxMenuItem(CheckboxMenuItem) method

Syntax: protected abstract CheckboxMenuItemPeer
                 createCheckboxMenuItem(CheckboxMenuItem target)

Description: The createCheckboxMenuItem(CheckboxMenuItem) method of the Toolkit
                 class creates a new checkbox menu item using a specified peer interface.
                 Creating a peer enables you to alter the on-screen appearance of a
                 checkbox menu item while retaining its original functionality. The target
                 parameter indicates the new checkbox menu item you want to create.

Toolkit

createChoice(Choice) method

Syntax: protected abstract ChoicePeer createChoice(Choice target)

Description: The createChoice(Choice) method of the Toolkit class creates a new choice (a drop-down menu of options that descends from a button) using a peer interface. Creating a peer enables you to alter the on-screen appearance of a choice while retaining its original functionality. The target parameter indicates the new choice you want to create.

createDialog(Dialog) method

Syntax: protected abstract DialogPeer createDialog(Dialog target)

Description: The createDialog(Dialog) method of the Toolkit class creates a new dialog box using a specified peer interface. Creating a peer enables you to alter the on-screen appearance of a dialog box while retaining its original functionality. The target indicates the new dialog box you want to create.

createFileDialog(FileDialog) method

Syntax: protected abstract FileDialogPeer createFileDialog(FileDialog target)

Description: The createFileDialog(FileDialog) method of the Toolkit class creates a new file dialog box (a dialog box that provides files from which to select) using a specified interface. Creating a peer enables you to alter the on-screen appearance of a file dialog box while retaining its original functionality. The target parameter indicates the new file dialog box you want to create.

createFrame(Frame) method

Syntax: protected abstract FramePeer createFrame(Frame target)

Description: The createFrame(Frame) method of the Toolkit class creates a new frame using a specified peer interface. Creating a peer enables you to alter the on-screen appearance of a frame while retaining its original functionality. The target parameter indicates the frame you want to create.

createImage(ImageProducer) method

Syntax: public abstract Image createImage(ImageProducer producer)

Description: The createImage(ImageProducer) method of the Toolkit class creates an image using a specified image producer (source). The producer parameter indicates the image producer (source) from which you want to derive the new image.

createLabel(Label) method

Syntax: protected abstract LabelPeer createLabel(Label target)

Description: The createLabel(Label) method of the Toolkit class creates a new text label for an object using a specified peer interface. Creating a peer enables you to alter the on-screen appearance of a text label while retaining its original functionality. The target parameter indicates the new label you want to create.

Toolkit

createList(List) method

Syntax: protected abstract ListPeer createList(List target)

Description: The createList(List) method of the Toolkit class creates a new list using a specified peer. Creating a peer enables you to alter the on-screen appearance of a text label while retaining its original functionality. The target parameter indicates the new list you want to create.

createMenu(Menu) method

Syntax: protected abstract MenuPeer createMenu(Menu target)

Description: The createMenu(Menu) method of the Toolkit class creates a new menu using a specified peer interface. Creating a peer enables you to alter the on-screen appearance of a menu while retaining its original functionality. The target parameter indicates the new menu you want to create.

createMenuBar(MenuBar) method

Syntax: protected abstract MenuBarPeer createMenuBar(MenuBar target)

Description: The createMenuBar(MenuBar) method of the Toolkit class creates a new menu bar using a specified peer interface. The target parameter indicates the new menu bar you want to create. Creating a peer enables you to alter the on-screen appearance of a menu bar while retaining its original functionality.

createMenuItem(MenuItem) method

Syntax: protected abstract MenuItemPeer createMenuItem(MenuItem target)

Description: The createMenuItem(MenuItem) method of the Toolkit class creates a new menu item using a specified peer interface. Creating a peer enables you to alter the on-screen appearance of a menu item while retaining its original functionality. The target parameter indicates the new menu item you want to create.

createPanel(Panel) method

Syntax: protected abstract PanelPeer createPanel(Panel target)

Description: The createPanel(Panel) method of the Toolkit class creates a new panel using a specified peer interface. Creating a peer enables you to alter the on-screen appearance of a panel while retaining its original functionality. The target a parameter indicates the new panel you want to create.

createScrollbar(Scrollbar) method

Syntax: protected abstract ScrollbarPeer createScrollbar(Scrollbar target)

Description: The createScrollbar(Scrollbar) method of the Toolkit class creates a new scrollbar using a specified peer interface. Creating a peer enables you to alter the on-screen appearance of a scrollbar while retaining its original functionality. The target parameter indicates the new scrollbar you want to create.

createTextArea(TextArea) method

Syntax: protected abstract TextAreaPeer createTextArea(TextArea target)

Description: The createTextArea(TextArea) method of the Toolkit class creates a new text area using a specified peer interface. Creating a peer enables you to alter the on-screen appearance of a text area while retaining its original functionality. The target parameter indicates the new text area you want to create.

createTextField(TextField) method

Syntax: protected abstract TextFieldPeer createTextField(TextField target)

Description: The createTextField(TextField) method of the Toolkit class creates a new text field using a specified peer interface. Creating a peer enables you to alter the on-screen appearance of a text field while retaining its original functionality. The target parameter indicates the new text field you want to create.

createWindow(Window) method

Syntax: protected abstract WindowPeer createWindow(Window target)

Description: The createWindow(Window) method of the Toolkit class creates a new window using a specified peer interface. Using a peer enables you to alter the on-screen appearance of a window while retaining its original function-ality. The target parameter indicates the new window you want to create.

getColorModel() method

Syntax: public abstract ColorModel getColorModel()

Description: The getColorModel() method of the Toolkit class determines the color scheme of a particular screen.

```
ColorModel cm =
➥Toolkit.getDefaultToolkit().getColorModel();
```

getDefaultToolkit() method

Syntax: public static synchronized Toolkit getDefaultToolkit()

Description: The getDefaultToolkit() method of the Toolkit class determines the default toolkit, which is controlled by the awt.toolkit property. When Java cannot locate the toolkit or the toolkit cannot be instantiated, the AWTError error is thrown.

```
ColorModel cm = Toolkit.getDefaultToolkit();
```

getFontList() method

Syntax: public abstract String[] getFontList()

Description: The getFontList() method of the Toolkit class returns a list of supported fonts for a particular platform.

```
String [] fontList = Toolkit.getDefaultToolkit().getFontList();
for (int index = 0; index < fontList.length; ++index) {
    System.out.println(fontList[index]);
}
```

getFontMetrics(Font) method

Syntax: public abstract FontMetrics getFontMetrics(Font f)

Description: The getFontMetrics(Font) method of the Toolkit class returns the screen metrics of a particular font. The font parameter indicates the font for which you want information.

```
FontMetrics myMetrics =
    Toolkit.getDefaultToolkit().getFontMetrics(myFont);
```

getImage(String) method

Syntax: public abstract Image getImage(String filename)

Description: The getImage(String) method of the Toolkit class accesses image pixel data from a specified file. The filename parameter indicates the file from which you want to retrieve the pixel data. This filename must be in one of the recognized file formats.

```
Image myImage =
➥Toolkit.getDefaultToolkit().getImage("test.gif");
```

getImage(URL) method

Syntax: public abstract Image getImage(URL url)

Description: The getImage(URL) method of the Toolkit class accesses image pixel data from a specified URL (Uniform Resource Locator). The URL parameter indicates the URL (resource locator) you want to use to locate data.

```
URL imageUrl = new URL(getDocumentBase(), "test.gif");
Image myImage = Toolkit.getDefaultToolkit().getImage(imageURL);
```

getScreenResolution() method

Syntax: public abstract int getScreenResolution()

Description: The getScreenResolution() method of the Toolkit class determines the screen resolution in dots-per-inch.

```
int res =
➥Toolkit.getDefaultToolkit().getScreenResolution();
```

getScreenSize() method

Syntax: public abstract Dimension getScreenSize()

Description: The getScreenSize() method of the Toolkit class determines the size of the screen in pixels.

Toolkit

```
Dimension d =
➥Toolkit.getDefaultToolkit().getScreenSize();
```

prepareImage(Image, int, int, ImageObserver) method

Syntax: public abstract boolean prepareImage(Image image, int width, int height, ImageObserver observer)

Description: The prepareImage(Image, int, int, ImageObserver) method of the Toolkit class prepares an image to appear on the default screen at the width and height you specify. The image parameter indicates the image you want to prepare for on-screen display. The width parameter indicates the width you want the image to be. The height parameter indicates the height you want the image to be. The observer parameter indicates whether the image is complete.

```
Toolkit.getDefaultToolkit().prepareImage(myImage, 300,
➥300, this);
```

sync() method

Syntax: public abstract void sync()

Description: The sync() method of the Toolkit synchronizes pending graphics so that they work together—a process that is highly useful when creating animations.

```
Toolkit.getDefaultToolkit().sync();
```

Window Class

Description: The Window class is one of the lesser, directly used classes in the awt toolkit. This class is part of the Container class and uses BorderLayout as its default layout manager. This class enables you to create top-level windows that contain no borders or menu bars. To create more complex windows, use the Frame or Dialog classes.

Constructors

Window(Frame) constructor

Syntax: public Window(Frame parent)

Description: The Window(Frame) constructor of the Window class creates a new window that begins in an invisible state and that behaves like a modal dialog box because it blocks input to other windows when it is on-screen. *Modal dialog boxes* are dialog boxes that accept user input. The parent parameter indicates the original window.

```
Window myWindow = new Window(parentFrame);
```

Window

Methods

addNotify() method

Syntax: public synchronized void addNotify()

Description: The addNotify() method of the Window class creates a peer of a particular window. Creating a peer enables you to alter the on-screen appearance of a window while retaining its original functionality.

dispose() method

Syntax: public synchronized void dispose()

Description: The dispose() method of the Window class deletes a particular window that is no longer essential. To release the system resources used by the discarded window, you must invoke this method.

```
myWindow.dispose();
```

getToolkit() method

Syntax: public Toolkit getToolkit()

Description: The getToolkit() method of the Window class determines the toolkit of a
particular frame.

```
Toolkit tk = myWindow.getToolkit();
```

getWarningString() method

Syntax: public final String getWarningString()

Description: The getWarningString() method of the Window class returns the warning
string for a particular window. Java displays warning strings on-screen in
windows that are not secure. The warning string will be null in application
windows. In windows opened by applets, the string will typically be
something like "Warning: Applet Window."

```
Frame topFrame = new Frame("Test");
topFrame.show();
System.out.println("Warning string is " +
➥topFrame.getWarningString());
```

Window

pack() method

Syntax: public synchronized void pack()

Description: The pack() method of the Window class packs (resizes) the window to
scale with the size of the components it contains.

```
Frame topFrame = new Frame("Test");
// ...
topFrame.pack();
topFrame.show();
```

show() method

Syntax: public synchronized void show()

Description: The show() method of the Window class displays a specified window.

```
Frame topFrame = new Frame("Test");
// ...
topFrame.show();
```

toBack() method

Syntax: public void toBack()

Description: The toBack() method of the Window class sends a frame to the back of (or behind) a particular window.

```
myWin.toBack();
```

toFront() method

Syntax: public void toFront()

Description: The toFront() method of the Window class displays a specified window on top of other windows.

```
myWin.toFront();
```

Window

INDEX

Symbols

3D rectangle objects
    creating, 180
    painting, 189
    see also image objects

A

ABORTED variable, MediaTracker class, 257
accessing
    checkboxes, 48
    menus from menu bars, 267
action(Event, Object) method, Component class, 70
ACTION_EVENT variable, Event class, 124
add(Component, int) method, Container class, 102-103
add(Component) method, Container class, 102
add(int, int) method, Rectangle class, 291
add(Menu) method, MenuBar class, 265
add(MenuItem) method, Menu class, 260
add(Point) method, Rectangle class, 291
add(Rectangle) method, Rectangle class, 292
add(String, Component) method, Container class, 103
add(String) method, Menu class, 260-261
addImage(Image, int, int, int) method, MediaTracker class, 248
addImage(Image, int) method, MediaTracker class, 248
adding
    components, 26
        to containers, 102-103
        to grid displays, 209
        to layout managers, 103
        to other components, 219
        to window card layouts, 35
        to window flow layouts, 148
    menu bars to menus, 265-266
    menu items, 54

points
    to polygon objects, 285
    to rectangle objects, 291
pull-down menu items, 260
rectangle objects to other rectangle objects, 292
scrolling list items, 233-234
separators to pull-down menus, 261
text strings to pull-down menu items, 260
addItem(String, int) method, List class, 234
addItem(String) method
    Choice class, 53
    List class, 233
addLayoutComponent(String, Component) method
    BorderLayout class, 26
    CardLayout class, 35
    FlowLayout class, 148
addLayoutComponent(String, Component) method, GridBagLayout class, 209, 219
addNotify() method
    Button class, 30
    Canvas class, 33
    Checkbox class, 43
    CheckboxMenuItem class, 51
    Choice class, 54
    Component class, 71
    Container class, 104
    Dialog class, 112
    FileDialog class, 142
    Frame class, 170
    Label class, 229
    List class, 234
    Menu class, 261
    MenuBar class, 266
    MenuItem class, 274
    Panel class, 279
    Scrollbar class, 300
    TextArea class, 310
    TextField class, 322
    Window class, 340

S

W

A VIACOM SERVICE

The Information SuperLibrary™

Bookstore

Search

What's New

Reference

Software

Newsletter

Company Overviews

Yellow Pages

Internet Starter Kit

HTML Workshop

Win a Free T-Shirt!

Macmillan Computer Publishing

Site Map

Talk to Us

CHECK OUT THE BOOKS IN THIS LIBRARY.

You'll find thousands of shareware files and over 1600 computer books designed for both technowizards and technophobes. You can browse through 700 sample chapters, get the latest news on the Net, and find just about anything using our massive search directories.

All Macmillan Computer Publishing books are available at your local bookstore.

We're open 24-hours a day, 365 days a year.

You don't need a card.

We don't charge fines.

And you can be as **LOUD** as you want.

The Information SuperLibrary
http://www.mcp.com/mcp/   ftp.mcp.com

Check Us Out Online!

New Riders has emerged as a premier publisher of computer books for the professional computer user. Focusing on CAD/graphics/multimedia, communications/internetworking, and networking/operating systems, New Riders continues to provide expert advice on high-end topics and software.

Check out the online version of *New Riders' Official World Wide Yellow Pages, 1996 Edition* for the most engaging, entertaining, and informative sites on the Web! You can even add your own site!

Hind Fire
Copyright 1995 - John Brooks

Brave our site for the finest collection of CAD and 3D imagery produced today. Professionals from all over the world contribute to our gallery, which features new designs every month.

From Novell to Microsoft, New Riders publishes the training guides you need to attain your certification. Visit our site and try your hand at the CNE Endeavor, a test engine created by VFX Technologies, Inc. that enables you to measure what you know—and what you don't!

New Riders

http://www.mcp.com/newriders

CHECK OUT THESE RELATED TOPICS OR SEE YOUR LOCAL BOOKSTORE

CAD

As the number one CAD publisher in the world, and as a Registered Publisher of Autodesk, New Riders Publishing provides unequaled content on this complex topic under the flagship *Inside AutoCAD*. Other titles include *AutoCAD for Beginners* and *New Riders' Reference Guide to AutoCAD Release 13*.

Networking

As the leading Novell NetWare publisher, New Riders Publishing delivers cutting-edge products for network professionals. We publish books for all levels of users, from those wanting to gain NetWare Certification, to those administering or installing a network. Leading books in this category include *Inside NetWare 3.12*, *Inside TCP/IP Second Edition*, *NetWare: The Professional Reference*, and *Managing the NetWare 3.x Server*.

Graphics and 3D Studio

New Riders provides readers with the most comprehensive product tutorials and references available for the graphics market. Best-sellers include *Inside Photoshop 3*, *3D Studio IPAS Plug In Reference*, *KPT's Filters and Effects*, and *Inside 3D Studio*.

Internet and Communications

As one of the fastest growing publishers in the communications market, New Riders provides unparalleled information and detail on this ever-changing topic area. We publish international best-sellers such as *New Riders' Official Internet Yellow Pages, 2nd Edition*, a directory of over 10,000 listings of Internet sites and resources from around the world, as well as *VRML: Browsing and Building Cyberspace, Actually Useful Internet Security Techniques, Internet Firewalls and Network Security*, and *New Riders' Official World Wide Web Yellow Pages*.

Operating Systems

Expanding off our expertise in technical markets, and driven by the needs of the computing and business professional, New Riders offers comprehensive references for experienced and advanced users of today's most popular operating systems, including *Inside Windows 95, Inside Unix, Inside OS/2 Warp Version 3*, and *Building a Unix Internet Server*.

Orders/Customer Service **1-800-653-6156**   Source Code **NRP95**

New Riders Publishing   201 West 103rd Street ◆ Indianapolis, Indiana 46290 USA

Name _____ Title _____

Company _____ Type of business _____

Address _____

City/State/ZIP _____

Have you used these types of books before? ☐ yes ☐ no

If yes, which ones? _____

_____

How many computer books do you purchase each year? ☐ 1–5 ☐ 6 or more

How did you learn about this book? _____

Where did you purchase this book? _____

Which applications do you currently use? _____

_____

Which computer magazines do you subscribe to? _____

_____

What trade shows do you attend? _____

_____

Comments: _____

_____

_____

Would you like to be placed on our preferred mailing list? ☐ yes ☐ no

☐ **I would like to see my name in print!** You may use my name and quote me in future New Riders products and promotions. My daytime phone number is: _____

New Riders Publishing   201 West 103rd Street ◆ Indianapolis, Indiana 46290 USA

Fax to **317-581-4670**   Orders/Customer Service **1-800-653-6156**   Source Code **NRP95**

Fold Here

- -

PLACE
STAMP
HERE

NEW RIDERS PUBLISHING
201 W 103RD ST
INDIANAPOLIS IN 46290-9058